THE TEMPLE OF THE LORD
AND OTHER STORIES

THE TEMPLE
OF THE LORD AND
OTHER STORIES

William A. Meninger, O.C.S.O.

with an introduction by
Theophane the Monk

CONTINUUM • NEW YORK

1997

The Continuum Publishing Company
370 Lexington Avenue
New York, NY 10017

Copyright © 1997 by William A. Meninger

Printed in the United States of America

Library of Congress Cataloging-in-Publication Data

Meninger, William.
     The Temple of the Lord and other stories / William A.
Meninger; with an introduction by Theophane the Monk.
          p.   cm.
     ISBN 0-8264-1062-6
     1. Temple of God—Meditations.   2. Wisdom (Biblical
personification)—Meditations.   3. Messiah—Meditations.
4. Jesus Christ—Messiahship—Meditations.   5. People
of God—Meditations.   6. Spiritual life—Catholic Church.
7. Catholic Church—Prayer–books and devotions—
English.   I. Title.
BS680. T4M46   1997
242—dc21   97–23225
                                                       CIP

Scripture quotations are from the *New International
Version* and the *New Oxford Annotated Bible*.

To Harold and Patricia Pabst and
to Ford and Susan Schumann
with affection and gratitude

Contents

Foreword

*Why did I go to the Magic Monastery?
Well, I'm a monk myself, and the strangest
thing happened in my monastery. We had a
visit from the Buddha. We prepared for it,
and gave him a very warm, though solemn,
welcome. He stayed overnight, but he
slipped away early in the morning, and
when we woke up we found graffiti all over
the cloister walls. Imagine! And do you
know what he wrote?*

*One word—TRIVIA-TRIVIA-TRIVIA—all over
the place.*

*Well, we were in a rage. But when I quieted
down, I looked about and realized, "Yes, it is
true." So much of what I saw was trivia, and
most of what I heard. But what is worse,
when I closed my eyes, all inside was trivia.
For several weeks this was my experience,
and my very efforts to rectify it just made it
worse. I left my monastery and headed for
the Magic Monastery. . . .*
                    —Tales of a Magic Monastery

TRIVIA—all over the place. Have you noticed? Inside, too? Not just in my monastery and inside my head? Nice book here. Addresses this plague.

In directing your own life, or in raising children, do you have some Temple of the Lord to which you can withdraw? There are plenty of churches around, but a Temple of the Lord? Do you know of one? Where is it? How much time do you spend there? What's it like? What do you do there? An altar there? Sacrifice? Hear some words? New words? Old words? Is it a physical place? What does the world look like when you come out? Would they let me in?

Father William, Trappist monk and scripture scholar, sets you up for some such reflection. In his first story, he recounts the development of the Temple tradition in the Old Testament, shows how, in the New Testament, Jesus embodies the Temple of God, and then how the theme refers to his followers; namely, us.

His second story is entitled "Wisdom Built a House." Wisdom? What have you found? Anything I can use? Anything your children can use? I have been seduced by trivia. Have you? Must we be seduced by trivia? Our whole lives long? Where is wisdom? I think I have enough intelligence, but where is wisdom? Fr. William traces this theme through the Old Testament, in the life of Jesus, and in its application to us.

His third story is entitled "Messiah of God." Do we have any responsibility in the face of this plague of trivia, foolishness, and spurious wisdom? We are reawakening to responsibility in regard to the environment, hunger, and social injustice. Fr. William's third story is about the Messiah, that is, the Anointed One, anointed for mature action. There's the theme of Messiah in the Old Testament, then Jesus as Messiah, but then the anointing of his followers for mature action, for responsibility—the anointing with the Spirit of God. Us it means.

Go ahead. Read it. Or, better, let the stories read you.

Theophane the Monk
St. Benedict's Monastery
Snowmass, CO

CHAPTER 1

The Temple of the Lord

Remember, O Lord, in David's favor,
  all the hardships he endured;
how he swore to the Lord
  and vowed to the Mighty One of Jacob,
"I will not enter my house
  or get into my bed;
I will not give sleep to my eyes
  or slumber to my eyelids,
until I find a place for the Lord,
  a dwelling place for the Mighty
    One of Jacob."

Lo, we heard of it in Ephrathah,
  we found it in the fields of Jaar.
"Let us go to his dwelling place;
  let us worship at his footstool!"

Arise, O Lord, and go to thy resting place,
  thou and the ark of thy might.
Let thy priests be clothed with righteousness,
  and let thy saints shout for joy.
For thy servant David's sake do not turn
  away from the face of thy anointed one.
                              —Ps. 132, 1–10

ONCE UPON A TIME, there was a Temple. I begin this way, because I want to share with you the story of the Lord's Temple. Not its history, but its story. If I dealt with the Temple's history, I would have to get involved with lots of dates, archeological data, and scholarly controversies. I deal, instead, with the Temple's story. This will free me—and you—to be selective, emotional, and even, to some degree, simple. This story, like all stories, is true, and like all stories, it embraces both the storyteller and the listeners.

There has not been a Temple of the Lord for more than nineteen hundred years, so I suppose it is really accurate to say, "Once upon a time there *was* a Temple." But there was also a time *before* there was a Temple, and it is to this time we must go to begin our story.

The time is some 1200 years before Christ. The people are the Hebrews, once slaves in Egypt, but now recently delivered under Yahweh's providence and Moses' leadership. The place is the stark, arid, mountainous peninsula of Sinai and the destitute desert lands of the Negev in southern Palestine. The story is not as simple as the Bible would have it. (Note that the Bible also tells stories rather than histories.) The Hebrews who eventually entered the Holy Land under the generalship of Joshua were not only that group of people who left Egypt with Moses. In their storied wanderings, they were joined by other Semitic-related peoples. As you would expect, these other peoples or tribes, as we call them, brought their own customs, stories, and theologies. Yes, they brought their own understandings of God and their own unique ways of relating to God.

One of these tribes, and it does not matter which, carried with them on their nomadic journeys a sacred, portable tent. It was in this tent, they believed, that their lord dwelt. He traveled with them, was present to them, and even was available for consultations with their priests and leaders. This tent we call a tabernacle. The meaning is the same.

Yet another tribe carried with them an ark. This actually served the same purpose as the tabernacle. It was a box, not a very large one, which could be carried on the shoulders of four priests. Certain sacred, cultic objects were carried inside this box, but, more importantly, their lord was present over it. You see, on top of this box or ark there were the figures of two angels, kneeling back to back, with their large wings touching. At the point where these wings touched, their lord dwelt to be present to and receive the praises of his people and even to lead them into battle.

The two tribes, along with some others, joined together and eventually formed a loosely united nation. At first, they were distinctly tribal, united not politically but religiously, in the sense that they worshipped a common god who they acknowledged had brought them to Palestine. Then, especially under King David and King Solomon, they became a strong, centrally oriented kingdom looking eventually to Jerusalem as their political and religious center. It was at this point that the two presences of the lord, in the tabernacle and above the ark having been fused, as it were, many years previously, found their home in the Temple of Jerusalem.

King David conquered Jerusalem about one thousand years before Christ. He saw its potential as a place to rally and politically unify twelve semi-independent tribal entities. He built himself there a magnificent palace. Then he said to his personal prophet, Nathan, "See now, I am living in a house of cedar, but the ark of God stays in a tent" (2 Sm. 7, 2).

David had brought the ark of the covenant with him to Jerusalem. Once it had actually been captured by the Philistine army, but it caused them great problems in the form of fatal accidents, plagues, and the destruction of their principal idols. Finally, they begged the Israelites to take it back, even giving them a kind of reverse ransom of gold as a guilt offering.

Amidst great rejoicing and fanfare, the ark was brought to Jerusalem and housed in its tabernacle. Later, in response to a plague in the city, David purchased a large stone-based threshing floor from one of the original Jebusite inhabitants to erect an altar of sacrifice. This threshing floor can be seen to this day beneath the golden Dome of the Rock on Mt. Sion. It was at this place the Temple of Yahweh was eventually to be built and where the tabernacle with its ark was to find a home.

King David greatly desired to build this temple, which would be the permanent dwelling place of the Lord in the midst of his people. He even wrote a song about it.

> O, Lord remember in David's favor all the hardships he endured; how he swore to the Lord and vowed to the Mighty One of Jacob,
> "I will not enter my house or get into my bed:
> I will not give sleep to my eyes or slumber to my eyelids, until I find a place for the Lord, a dwelling place for the Mighty One of Jacob."

... Rise up, O Lord and go to your resting place, you and the ark of your might.

... For the Lord has chosen Zion; he has desired it for his habitation: [Yahweh said,] "This is my resting place forever: here will I reside, for I have desired it." (Ps. 132)

But it was not to be. God spoke to the prophet Nathan in a dream and said, "Go and tell my servant David: Thus says the Lord: Are you the one to build me a house to live in? I have not lived in a house since the day I brought up the people of Israel from Egypt to this date, but I have been moving about in a tent" (2 Sm. 7, 5f.). Then Yahweh went on to tell David that the house David was to build would be a house of living stones, of offspring "who shall come forth from your body." It would be the duty and the privilege of David's son and heir to the throne, Solomon, to build the Temple of the Lord.

One day after David saw that his kingdom was secure and that his wealth was equal to the task, he summoned together:

All the officials of Israel, the officials of the tribes, the officers of the divisions that served the king, the commanders of the thousands, the commanders of the hundreds, the stewards of all the property and cattle of the king and his sons, together with the palace officials, the mighty warriors and all the warriors. Then King David rose to his feet and said: "Hear me, my brothers and my people. I had planned to build a house of rest for the ark of the covenant of the Lord, for the footstool of our God; and I made preparations for building. But God said to me, 'You shall not build a house for my name, for you are a warrior and have shed blood.' . . . He said to me, 'It is your son Solomon who shall build my house and my courts. . .' " (1 Ch. 28, 1–6)

Then, in the midst of that solemn gathering, David commissioned his son to build the Temple with these words: "Take heed now, for the Lord has chosen you to build a house as the sanctuary; be strong and act" (1 Ch. 28, 10). Although he couldn't build the Lord's house himself, David wanted it to be known that he was the one behind it. Only in this way could he fulfill his vow "to find a place for the Lord, a dwelling place for the mighty one of Jacob" (Ps. 132). And so he gave to Solomon the plans for the Temple," and of its houses, its treasures, its upper rooms, and its inner chambers, and of the room for the mercy seat" (1 Ch. 28, 11). The mercy seat was on the ark of the covenant over which the Lord's presence hovered. He also presented him with the treasury needed for the golden vessels of the altar, to pay for the services of the priests and "his plan for the golden Chariot of the Cherubim that spread their wings and covered the ark of the covenant of the Lord" (vs. 18).

After a reign of 40 years, King David slept with his ancestors and was buried in Jerusalem at the very spot where, a thousand years later, Jesus was to establish a new covenant sealed with the sacrifice of his body and blood at the Last Supper. So Solomon sat on the throne of his father David by whose wisdom and the favor of the Lord his kingdom was firmly established.

Solomon's historian grandly announces the commencement of the Temple building in these words. "In the four hundred eightieth year after the Israelites came out of the land of Egypt, in the fourth year of Solomon's reign over Israel, in the month of Zio, which is the second month, he began to build the house of the lord" (1 Kgs. 6, 1). It took 7 years to complete and the account of its building is truly the stuff out of which stories are made.

Thirty thousand men were sent to level the forests of Lebanon for cedar. Seventy thousand laborers and eighty thousand stone cutters were sent to the quarries in the hill country. These vast crews labored under the supervision of thirty-three hundred foremen. The stones were hewn to shape in the quarries, and the cedar beams were prefabricated "so that neither hammer nor ax nor any tool of iron was heard in the temple while it was being built" (1 Kg. 6, 7).

When the Temple was ready, Solomon assembled the elders of Israel and the leaders of their ancestral houses and commanded the priests to bring up the ark of the Lord and the tabernacle with all its holy vessels and to place them in the most holy place built as the focal point of the Temple. (There they would remain in a darkened room whose entrance was covered by a heavy veil. No one was to enter this Holy of Holies except the high priest once a year.). Then the priests offered in sacrifice so many sheep and oxen that they could not be counted or numbered.

At this point, the story tells us, Solomon preached a long and ominous sermon. He told them that Yahweh (Blessed be He!) had chosen the tribes of Israel to be his people. He now dwelt in a house in their midst. His real dwelling was in the heavens, but this Temple would be the place where he would heed their prayers. He would stay with them as long as they obeyed his commandments, honored his name, prayed to him for their daily needs, their defense in war, and in sorrow for their sins, "for there is no one who does not sin." Solomon ended with this prayer.

> Blessed be the Lord who has given rest to his people Israel. According to all he promised: not one word has failed of all his good promise, which he spoke through his servant Moses. The Lord our God be with us as he was with our ancestors; may he not leave us or abandon us, but incline our hearts to him, to walk in all his ways, and to keep his commandments, his statutes, and his ordinances which he commanded our ancestors. . . . Therefore devote yourselves completely to the Lord our Lord, walking in his statutes and keeping his commandments, as at this day. (1 Kgs. 8, 56–61)

No doubt King Solomon was very sincere when he offered this prayer. A short time later he was to learn that Yahweh (Blessed be He!) took it very seriously, indeed, because he appeared to Solomon in the privacy of his chambers and said,

> I have heard your prayer and your plea, which you made before me. I have consecrated this house which you have built and put my name there forever; my eyes and my heart will be there for all time. . . . If you turn aside from following me, you or your children and do not keep my commandments . . . then I will cut Israel off from the land that I have given them and the house that I have consecrated. This house will become a heap of ruins. . . . (1 Kgs. 9, 6–8)

It is the tragedy of this Temple story that that threatening prophecy was to be fulfilled. Even today, when the Orthodox Rabbis in Israel speak of the destruction of the Temple, they say that it occurred because God's people had sinned, and there is no new Temple, because the people are not worthy of it. They base this claim on those very words that Yahweh spoke to Solomon.

To continue the story of the Temple—things went well for a while, but only for a while. Solomon's Temple suffered from all the troubles that afflicted the nation itself. It was altered, desecrated, restored, and eventually reduced to rubble even as the political entity of Israel was changed, desecrated, restored, and destroyed.

King Ahaz sold some of the Temple's bronze furnishing to pay tribute to the Assyrians. King Josiah in the seventh century B.C., during a period of national independence, began a great religious reform centering on Temple worship and national fidelity to Yahweh. But it did not last. Too much emphasis was placed on the presence of God in the Holy of Holies, and too little deference was given to the observance of his commands. The prophets were sent to warn the people not to put their confidence in a building, no matter how holy.

Things went from bad to worse, and there were even periods when the temple was used for pagan worship and housed idols "made by human hands." Shortly before the Babylonians destroyed Solomon's Temple in 587 B.C., the prophet Ezekiel was given the tragic task of a final warning. The spirit of Yahweh (Blessed be He!) grabbed him by his hair and carried him up between heaven and Earth and brought him to Jerusalem from his exile in Babylon.

> He said to me, "Go in [to the Temple], and see the vile abominations that they are committing here." So I went in and looked; there, portrayed on the wall all around, were all kinds of creeping things, and loathsome animals, and all the idols of the house of Israel. (Ez. 8, 10)

Ezekiel saw standing before these idols, the seventy elders of Israel each one offering incense and saying, "Yahweh does not see us. Yahweh has forsaken the land."

It was time for the Lord to fulfill his threats. His people had brought it upon themselves. Shortly after this vision, the Babylonian army destroyed the city of Jerusalem, its walls, and its Temple. All the significant people, the politicians, the teachers, wealthy merchants, artisans, military leaders, and priests were marched away into exile. The wealth of the Temple was taken. The building and its altars were destroyed. The Lord no longer dwelt in the midst of his people. "They burned the house of God, broke down the wall of Jerusalem, burned all its palaces with fire, and destroyed all its precious vessels" (2 Chr. 36, 19).

It is time for a flashback in our story of the Temple. This Babylonian exile was neither the first nor the worst the Israelites had endured. About 300 years after Solomon built the Temple, after the country had split into two kingdoms, Israel in the north and Judah in the south, the Assyrian army descended from the north and conquered the northern Kingdom of Israel. In 721, they captured the capital city, Samaria, and following the customary policy, took into exile all of the significant leaders of the ten tribes that constituted the northern kingdom of Israel. In their place, they brought in another captive people who would not be inclined to rebel against Assyrian rule in a country not their own. It was here that there began the many storied accounts of the "ten lost tribes of Israel." These newcomers of course, were not Jews, but pagans.

However, over the next 200 years, they became assimilated with those Jews who were allowed to remain in the north. They even adopted, after their own fashion, the religion of the native Jews. They were never accepted politically, religiously, or socially by the remaining "real" Jews in the southern kingdom of Judah. This situation was to become very significant in the subsequent story of the Temple.

Unlike the Assyrian exile of 721, which was permanent, the Babylonian exile was to last only 50 years. It became a period of intense religious activity for the exiles, who were allowed considerable freedom (although not without some persecution) to follow their religion. They longed for a return to Jerusalem and made heroic efforts to retain their distinct nationality and religious observances. One particularly poignant song from that period goes like this:

> By the rivers of Babylon—
>   there we sat down there we wept
>   when we remembered Zion.
> On the willows there we hung up our harps
> For there our captors asked us for songs,

and our tormentors asked for mirth
saying, "Sing us one of the songs of Zion!"

How could we sing the Lord's song
in a foreign land?
If I forget you, O Jerusalem,
let my right hand wither!
Let my tongue cling to the roof of my mouth,
if I do not remember you, if I do not set
Jerusalem above my highest joy. (Ps. 137, 1–6)

After 50 years in exile, the Judeans (whom we will call the people of the southern Kingdom of Judah) were allowed to return home by the conqueror of the Babylonians, Cyrus, King of Persia. We have the very text of the decree by which Cyrus permitted the Judeans residing in Babylon to return to Jerusalem and rebuild the city and its Temple.

Thus says King Cyrus of Persia: the Lord the God of heaven has given me all the kingdoms of the earth, and he has charged me to build him a house at Jerusalem in Judah. Any of those among you who are his people—may their God be with them—are now permitted to go up to Jerusalem in Judah, and rebuild the house of the Lord, the God of Israel—he is the God who is in Jerusalem; and let all survivors, in whatever place they reside, be assisted by the people of their place with silver and gold, with goods and with animals, besides freewill offerings for the House of God in Jerusalem. (Ezr. 1, 2–4)

And so the Temple was rebuilt. Once again the Holy of Holies, the place where God's glory resided was restored to his people. This time, however, it was without the Ark or the Tent, which, tradition tells us, were brought to Mt. Sinai and sealed, together with the altar of incense, in a hidden cave at a place that "shall remain unknown until God gathers his people together again and shows his mercy" (2 Mc. 2, 7). We will not see the Ark again until the seventh angel blows his trumpet and reveals "God's temple in heaven was opened and the ark of his covenant was seen within his temple" (Rev. 11, 19), and round about it there were flashes of lightning, peals of thunder, and earthquakes. Even without the Ark and the historic tabernacle, the people were content to know that God resided once again in the Holy of Holies enthroned now "upon the praises of Israel."

Construction of the Second Temple was began in 537 B.C. We know little of the details of its architecture but assume that it was rebuilt along the lines of the First Temple. It took longer to build, however, because of problems with the neighboring Samaritans.

I have already told you their story. They considered themselves, of course, to be every bit as Jewish as the Judeans and expected to take their rightful part in the rebuilding of the new Temple. Their offers were scornfully repudiated by the returned exiles, so they went back to Samaria and built their own temple on Mt. Gerizim near the modern city of Nablus.

At this point, it would be good for me to divert a little and to tell you some more of their story, because we shall meet them again. It was only a short time ago, in 1995, that the ruins of their temple were unearthed. It was seen to be built according to the plans of the Jerusalem Temple. This Samaritan temple was destroyed by Jewish forces in 128 B.C. The site of the temple was still used for worship in Jesus' time even without the building.

Three years after the crucifixion of Jesus, Pontius Pilate massacred the Samaritans. It was this that was responsible for his recall to Rome. The remaining Samaritans rebuilt again and made a stand on Mt. Gerizim. They were severely weakened by lack of water, and the Roman army stormed their mountains and killed the entire force that had refused to surrender.

A remnant of Samaritans exists to this day— about 200 of them—still separate from the Jews and still offering their own worship to Yahweh on Mt. Gerizim. They await a Messiah whom they call The Restorer. Refusing to recognize the offspring of "mixed marriages" as true Samaritans, they are doomed to extinction in the not-too-distant future.

As is so often the case between close blood relatives, the relationship between the Jews and the Samaritans was bitter and hateful. It is even believed that the Jewish insistance on genealogies (such as we see for Jesus in the infancy narratives) was to prove that they had no taint of Samaritan blood.

In his controversy with the Judeans shortly before his death, Jesus told them they do not hear God's word "because whoever is from God hears the words of God. The reason you do not hear them is that you are not from God" (Jn. 8, 47). Listen to their angry response, "Are we not right in saying that you are a Samaritan and have a demon?" (vs. 48). As far as they were concerned, one included the other. Jesus, however, refused to accept this correspondence of demon and Samaritan by denying that he had a demon and refusing even to acknowledge the accusation of being a Samaritan, because he replied simply, "I do not have a demon, but I honor my Father" (vs. 49).

The antagonism between Jew and Samaritan extended into every way of life. Because of their geographical location, between Judea (and Jerusalem) in the south and the Galilee in the north, the normal route for Galileans in their thrice yearly visits to the Temple in Jerusalem would take them through Samaritan territory. The journey from Galilee normally took 3 days. The Samaritans made this pilgrimage very difficult for the Jews (including such devout pilgrims as Jesus, Mary, and Joseph), refusing them hospitality and deliberately presenting such obstacles as they could. As a result, Jews from the north usually took a longer, more round-about route to Jerusalem, going down to the Jordan Valley and following the river almost to the Dead Sea, turning west at Jericho to take the road "up to Jerusalem."

From all this, we can now understand how powerful, dramatic, and difficult was Jesus' teaching on love of neighbor as presented in the parable of the Good Samaritan. Probably returning to the north from Jerusalem, a Jew was "going down to Jericho" when he was attacked by robbers and left for dead. His own people in the persons of a priest and a Levite (a member of the priestly tribe) passed by, ignoring him. It was finally a Samaritan, a detested member of that very group whose enmity was probably responsible in the first place for the Jew to be on the road to Jericho, who cared for him, nursed his wounds, and carried him to shelter with a guarantee for any future care that might be needed. When Jesus asked his listeners who was the real loving neighbor of the wounded man, they could not even bring themselves to say the detested name, Samaritan, but replied "He who showed him mercy." It was a very hard thing, indeed, for them to accept.

Let us get back now to our story of the Temple, that is, the Second Temple. Because of Samaritan interference, it took 22 years to build and was finally completed in 515 B.C. The finished building, although lacking the glitter of its predecessor, was significant and worthy of its noble function.

For the next 300 years, things went up and down, for better and for worse, in the ongoing story of the Temple. When the Greeks conquered the region 200 years before Christ, not only their culture, but their religion dominated the minds and hearts of the Judeans. What happened then to the Temple was the result of their own folly.

> The Greek ruler, Antiochus, went up against Israel and came to Jerusalem with a strong force. He arrogantly entered the sanctuary and took the golden altar, the lampstand for the light and all its utensils. He also took the table for the bread of the Presence, the cups for drink offerings, the bowls, the golden censers, the curtain, the crowns, and the golden decoration on the front of the temple; he stripped it all off. He took the silver and the gold, and the costly vessels; he took also the hidden treasures that he found. Taking them all, he went into his own land . . . and all the house of Jacob was clothed with shame. (1 Mac. 1, 20–29)

Again, things went from bad to worse, when a few years later in 167 B.C., the sacrifices proscribed by the Torah were forbidden, and the Temple became the center for the pagan cult of Zeus Olympus. It was said that even pigs were sacrificed on Yahweh's holy altar.

How low God's people had sunk and how shamefully they allowed the Holy Presence in the Holy of Holies to be desecrated! It was indeed a far cry from the love songs once lyrically offered on Temple festivals by the chorus of maidens and the Levites, as recorded in the hymnbook of the Second Temple, which we call the Psalter.

> O Lord, I love the house in which you dwell, and the place where your glory dwells. (Ps. 26,8)
> . . . One thing I asked of the Lord that will I seek after: to live in the house of the Lord all the days of my life, to behold the beauty of the Lord and to inquire in his temple. (Ps. 27, 4)
> How lovely is your dwelling place, O Lord of hosts! My soul longs, indeed it faints for the courts of the Lord; my heart and my flesh sing for joy to the living God.
> Even the sparrow finds a home and the swallow a nest for herself where she may lay her young at your altars
> O Lord of hosts, my King and my God
> Happy are those who live your house ever singing your praise. (Ps. 84, 1–4)

Remembering and, no doubt, inspired by such national love songs for the Temple and the presence of the Lord, a strong and devout family of brothers, called the Maccabees, rose from the suppressed Jewish nation. Both military and priestly in background, these zealous patriots conquered the Greek overlords and, persuaded that Judaism could not survive without the Temple as a focus, rededicated the desecrated house of worship. The memorial of that rededication is celebrated by Jews to this day on the Feast of Hanukkah.

Shortly after the Greeks were ousted, it was the Romans' turn to dominate the tiny land of the Judeans. They contributed their own brand of desecration to the Temple by setting up in its presence their military standards with their idolatrous graven images and by actually entering into the forbidden sanctum of the Holy of Holies. This would later be referred to as "the abomination of desolation" in the memory of national shame and outrage.

But now in the tale of the Temple a great beacon of light began to shine. Herod the Great, appointed king by the Emperor in Rome, in order to remove the hostility the Judeans felt toward him as being only a "half-Jew," began in the year 20 B.C. the construction of a new magnificent Temple. He spared no expense in producing a luxurious temple complex. Ten thousand men worked for 10 years on the construction. One thousand priests from the tribe of Levi were trained as masons so they could work on the most sacred sections of the Holy Place and the Holy of Holies. The building was completed in 10 years, but the work of decoration was carried on until 64 A.D., 44 years from the inauguration of this enormous undertaking and only 6 years before this edifice, called the most magnificent building in the Empire, was to be totally demolished by the Roman army.

In the year 70 A.D. all of the threats, all of the dire forecasts, all of the warnings of the prophets were to descend upon the Judeans through the cataclysmic force of the Roman army. Because of a rebellion and as an example to the entire Empire, the city of Jerusalem, its walls and its magnificent Temple were utterly destroyed.

> I will utterly sweep away everything from the face of the earth, says the Lord.
> I will sweep away humans and animals;
> I will sweep away the birds of the air and the fish of the sea.
> I will make the wicked stumble
> I will cut off humanity from the face of the earth, says the Lord
> I will stretch out my hands against Judah and against all the inhabitants of Jerusalem.
> (Zeph. 1, 2–4)

No longer did the people of God, now scattered far and wide, sing love songs to the House of God. Wherever small groups of the faithful fearfully gathered to observe the Sabbath, the air was rent with the wailings of their lamentations:

> How lonely sets the city that once was full of people!
> How like a widow she has become, she that was great among the nations! . . .
> She weeps bitterly in the night with tears on her cheeks . . .
> She has no one to comfort her.
> The roads to Zion mourn, for no one comes to the festivals; All her gates are desolate, her priests groan.

> Her foes have become the masters, her enemies
> prosper, because the Lord has made her suffer for
> the multitude of her transgressions . . .
> Enemies have stretched out their hands over all
> her precious things,
> She has even seen the nations invade her
> sanctuary, those whom you forbade to enter
> your congregation
> Is it nothing to you, all you who pass by?
> Look and see if there is any sorrow like my sorrow
> Which was brought upon me
> Which the Lord inflicted on the day of his fierce
> anger. (Lam. ch.1)

The Temple, the Holy of Holies, where God was enthroned upon the praises of Israel, was gone! But always in the hearts and hopes of the Jewish people now scattered throughout the world echoed the promises of a merciful God.

> Thus says the Lord:
> I am going to restore the fortunes of the tents of
> Jacob, And have compassion on his dwellings,
> the city shall be rebuilt on its mound,
> and the citadel set on its rightful site.
> Out of them shall come thanksgiving,
> and the sound of merrymakers. (Jer. 31, 18–19)

But how is this to be? The story of the Temple came to a crashing conclusion engineered by the fury of Roman wrath so that there did not remain a stone upon a stone. Oh, it is true that briefly in the third century, the Roman Emperor gave the scattered Jews permission to return to Jerusalem and rebuild their Temple. They were gathering materials and funds and summoning the remnants of the tribe of Levi when the project was aborted by a new Roman decree. Then for fifteen hundred years almost nothing is heard about the Temple except that implied by the yearly yearning plea uttered by exiled Jews throughout the world at the conclusion of their Passover seders, "Next year, in Jerusalem!"

There are stories, many of them, expressing the grief the loss of the Temple imposed. Indeed, to this very day among Orthodox Jews, a commemorative day of mourning is held annually. One woefully dramatic tale comes to us from the Diaspora (scattered Jews) of the Middle Ages. According to the story, the Spirit of Yahweh one day decided to return to Mount Sion to seek out her rightful place on the Mercy seat of the Ark in the Holy of Holies. The night air was filled with the banshee-like wailing of her cries as she flitted from place to place frantically seeking her Temple sanctuary, which she could not find because it was not. Only when the people are worthy of it, the rabbis teach, will the Temple be restored.

One of the most dramatic events in Temple history occurred in Jerusalem on the Temple Mount in the seventh century, A.D. Jerusalem was conquered again by invaders. This time it was the unstoppable flood of Muslim soldiers marching north from the Arabian Peninsula. For 600 years, mostly under Christian disdain for the Old Testa-ment, Mt. Sion, the site of the Temple, had been used as a garbage heap. When the Muslim leader, the Sherif, saw this desecration of the sacred place, he ordered his soldiers to bring, under arms, the Christian Patriarch of Jerusalem and two shovels. Handing a shovel to the

Patriarch and wielding the other himself, he began the work of clearing the Temple Mount.

Their labor inaugurated what was to be called the most beautiful building in the world, the Dome of the Rock, a Muslim shrine, built on the site of the Temple of Solomon. It remains to this day, after Mecca and Medina, the third holiest Muslim shrine in the world. According to Islam, it is a worthy successor to the Temple, according to Jews, it is an abomination.

When the Crusaders conquered the Holy Land for a brief reign of 100 years in the thirteenth century, the Dome was consecrated as a cathedral for Catholic worship. After the Crusader defeat, it was returned to Muslim hands and remains so today under the official protection of the King of Jordan, although it is in Israeli-claimed territory.

Under detailed restrictions and careful scrutiny of Arab guards, the Temple Mount is open today to non-Muslim visitors, even to Israelis-Jews, whose military presence is all too obvious on the periphery of the sacred precincts. However, on the large ramp next to the wailing wall, which is the main entrance for non-Muslims, there is a large sign in Hebrew that forbids, by order of the Jerusalem Rabbinate, any Jew from entering the Temple area. This is because the exact site of the Holy of Holies is not known, and there is a fear that some Jew, other than the High Priest, might inadvertently step on that sacred spot.

Just a stone's throw from the Temple area is a restored Jewish synagogue where guides will point out a glass shelf before a high window looking toward Mt. Sion that holds a vase of oil being kept for the consecration of the altar of sacrifice when the Temple is rebuilt. On the window itself is painted a rainbow, a symbol of God's promise to his people, "When I bring clouds over the earth and the rainbow is seen in the clouds, I will remember my covenant that is between me and you" (Gn. 9, 14–15).

Nearby, in the newly built Jewish Quarter of the Old City are artisans' shops displaying the priestly vestments and the vessels of the altar ready for use when the Temple is restored. In the very heart of the Muslim Quarter, south of the Temple Mount, is a synagogue whose members are mostly young Israeli soldiers. It is well known that they are not content to wait until the people are worthy to restore the Temple. They are prepared at a moment's notice to advance on the Dome of the Rock and take the sacred precincts by force.

But what does all this mean? Has the Presence of God in his holy place disappeared from the Earth forever? Is the Dome of the Rock now the Holy of Holies? What does this mean to Christians?

To continue this fascinating story of the Temple of the Lord, we must now look at another manifestation of God's presence on earth, at the Word that was made flesh and who dwelt in our midst, Jesus the Christ. How very interesting it is to see that the entire life of Jesus on this Earth was dominated by the Temple. Herod's reconstruction began shortly before his birth. It was substantially finished during his adult life and was the center of his activities whenever he was in Jerusalem.

It was not the place where the presence of Emmanuel, God-is-with-us, was first shown to an expectant world. This was to take place only 6 miles away in a simple structure built for animals in Bethlehem. But it was at the Temple that Jesus was to be presented by his parents and where he would receive an "official" recognition by the prophets Simeon and Anna. The Temple was where he belonged. It was his father's house! As a child of twelve he expected Joseph and Mary to realize this. When they sought him for 3 days believing him to be lost, he was found in the Temple. He chided them for having to search for him. Where else could he be but in his father's house? Because he took to himself the words of Ps. 69, "It is zeal for your house that has consumed me; the insults of those who insult you have fallen on me," Jesus drove the money changers from the Temple. The house of prayer was being turned into a market place, even a den of thieves.

In the time of Jeremiah, during the period of Solomon's Temple, the people were strongly condemned for placing their confidence in God's presence in the Temple and ignoring his commandments.

> Thus says the Lord of hosts, the God of Israel: Amend your ways and your doings, and let me dwell with you in this place. Do not trust in these deceptive words: "This is the temple of the Lord, the temple of the Lord, the temple of the Lord."

It seems that this is just what one of the disciples was doing one day as he was leaving the Temple with Jesus. "Look, Teacher," he said, "What large stones and what large buildings" (Mk. 13, 1). Jesus' reply shows that the disciple was putting too much emphasis on the material element of the Temple. He answered, "Do you see these great buildings? Not one stone will be left upon another; all will be thrown down."

Yes, Jesus knew that the Temple was his Father's house but it seems that a new knowledge grew within him as he advanced in age, wisdom, and grace. When he drove the money changers from the Temple, Jesus again referred to the Temple as his father's house. When the people demanded that he show some sign that would prove his authority to discipline such abuses, Jesus answered them, "Destroy this Temple and in 3 days I will raise it up." The Judeans, of course, were indignant, because they knew that Herod had been for 46 years endeavoring to put up this huge structure. Jesus was claiming the ability to reconstruct it, if it were destroyed, in 3 days! The Gospel of John tells us:

> But he was speaking of the temple of his body. After he was raised from the dead, his disciples remembered that he had said this, and they believed the scripture and the word that Jesus had spoken. (Jn. 2, 22)

And here we have for the first time, a direct reference to the successor of Herod's Temple! Here we have the bold, incredible statement that the presence of God among his people was to be found in Jesus. The Body of Christ was the Temple of the Lord. Jesus proved by his resurrection that he was truly Emmanuel, God-is-with-us!

But, what of the presence of God in the Holy of Holies enthroned upon the praises of Israel? Even

before the material destruction of the building 37
years after the Resurrection, God had deserted it. His
presence was to be seen, felt, honored, and revealed in
the body of Christ and in all the mystical and concrete, supernatural and tangible realities that mystery embodies.

Just minutes before Jesus entered into the
prophetic sign we know as his death and resurrection
event, the presence of Yahweh departed from the
Temple, St. Luke tells us," and darkness came over
the whole land until three in the afternoon, when the
sun's light failed and the curtain of the temple was
torn in two." St. Mark adds that it was torn "from
top to bottom." This refers to the curtain spoken of
in the Book of Exodus,

> You shall make a curtain of blue, purple and crim-
> son yarns, and of fine twisted linen. It shall be made
> with Cherubim skillfully worked into it . . . you
> shall hang the curtain under the clasps, and bring
> the ark of the covenant in there, within the curtain;
> and the curtain shall separate for you the holy place
> from the most holy. You shall put the mercy seat
> on the ark of the covenant in the most holy place
> [Holy of Holies]. (Ex. 26, 33–34)

The unthinkable had happened. The Holy of
Holies was exposed to the profane eyes of the entire
world with the rendering of its protective curtain and
God had departed from his mercy seat. This depar-
ture was simultaneous with the death of Jesus. St.
Matthew makes this very clear when he says "Jesus
cried again with a loud voice and breathed his last. *At
that moment* [emphasis mine] the curtain of the
temple was torn in two" (Mt. 27, 51).

There was a sense then that from the time of Jesus' death, God was absent from the midst of his people. His presence was to be restored by reason of the Resurrection. "Destroy this temple and in three days I will raise it up." "But he was speaking of the Temple of his body." This means, of course, that God's presence, being freed, as it were, from the constraints of the physical Temple was now to be seen, experienced, and even touched wherever the risen Christ was seen, experienced, or touched.

> We declare to you what was from the beginning, what we have heard, what we have seen with our eyes, what we have looked at and touched with our hands, concerning the word of life that was with the Father and was revealed to us—we declare to you what we have seen and heard so that you also may have fellowship with us; and truly our fellowship is with the Father and with his Son Jesus Christ. (1 Jn. 1, 1–4)

Two things happened with the rending of the veil of the Temple. First, God no longer dwelt there in the Holy of Holies. Second, God was now available not just through the agency of the high priest who approached the sanctuary once a year but through the one mediator Jesus Christ who is with us all days even to the end of time. He could now be experienced, seen, and touched through his body and blood, given up for us and embodied in us in the great mystery of the Lord's Supper. Because he was so embodied in his people, he would be present to them wherever two or three of them were assembled in his name. It is no longer a question of approaching God only once a year through the mediation of a high priest in fear and trembling as he enters the Holy of Holies; we now have "fellowship with the Father and with his son Jesus Christ."

Now we can understand what Jesus meant in his very unusual conversation with the Samaritan woman at Jacob's well. Jesus was tired from his journey coming south from Galilee and sat by the well to rest, while his disciples went into the nearby town of Sychar to buy food. The woman came to the well and Jesus asked her if she would draw him some water. The well was deep, the sun was high, and he had no equipment to get water.

The story in John ch. 6 does not tell us if the woman gave him some water. We would like to think she did. We do know that as a Samaritan, she would give Jesus, a Jew, a hard time. And she did. "You are a Jew and I am a Samaritan woman. How can you ask me for a drink?" And to remind us of the enmity between the two, St. John reminds the reader, "For Jews do not associate with Samaritans."

It did not take very long before the conversation turned to the ancient issue between Jews and Samaritans, the Temple. "Our fathers," she said, "worshipped on this mountain, but you Jews claim that the place where we must worship is in Jerusalem." Jesus' response summed up in one sentence the meaning of the whole story of the Temple of the Lord from its very beginning. "Believe me woman," he said, "a time is coming when you will worship the Father neither on this mountain nor in Jerusalem . . . a time is coming and has now come when the true worshipper will worship the Father in spirit and in truth for they are the kind of worshippers the Father seeks."

In a short time, the Temple in Jerusalem would no longer exist. Jerusalem would be destroyed by the Roman army. Its walls, its palaces, its citadels, and its Temple would be left almost without a stone upon a stone. The city would eventually be rebuilt but never the Temple.

In a siege under Generals Vespasian and Titus, both of whom would later become Roman emperors, and in fulfillment of a prophecy tearfully uttered by Jesus, all of the Temple and most of the city of Jerusalem were destroyed in the year 70. Another destruction, this time a virtual annihilation, would take place 60 years later. From that time on for centuries, it was forbidden for a Jew even to set foot in the city.

But what of Yahweh's promises. He had said to Solomon when the Temple was first completed, "I have heard your prayer and your plea, which you made before me. I have consecrated this house that you have built, and put my name there forever; my eyes and my heart will be there for all time" (1 Kgs. 9, 3). Well, we have seen, have we not, that God's eyes and heart will be with God's people forever in the loving eyes and the Sacred Heart of Jesus Christ. Wherever he is—and he is wherever two or three of his followers are assembled—Yahweh will be worshipped in spirit and in truth. Jesus is truly the Temple of the Lord!

But this is not all. There is more to our story and perhaps the most important part. When the Hebrew community under Moses had arrived, in their long journey from Egypt to Palestine, at Kadesh in the Desert of Zin, they were without water. It was so bad that many of them, including

Moses' sister Miriam, died. Moses and Aaron went
to the tabernacle where God dwelt over the ark and
fell on their faces. The glory of Yahweh appeared to
them saying;

> Take your staff, and assemble the congregation,
> you and your brother Aaron, and command the
> rock before their eyes to yield its water. Thus you
> shall bring water out of the rock for them. . . .
> Then Moses lifted up his hand and struck the rock
> twice with his staff, water came out abundantly,
> and the congregation and their livestock drank.
> (Num. 20, 7–11)

This wonderful act of God's mercy was com-
memorated each year in the Temple liturgy on the
Feast of Tabernacles. This feast had a special relationship to the Temple, because it was on this day that
Solomon dedicated the House of God. It was celebrated for 7 days. It was an agricultural feast, and
prayers for an abundance of rain fitted naturally into
the commemoration. Coming in early October, the
Feast of Tabernacles, even today, is a time when all
watch carefully to see if rain falls during that period. It
would be a good sign for the following year's harvest.

During the Second Temple, a solemn ceremony
dramatized the gift of water from Yahweh to his people. On each of the seven mornings of the feast, a
procession of priests went down to the Gihon springs
at the base of the Temple Mount. Here a priest filled
a golden pitcher with water as the choristers sang,
"With joy you will draw water from the wells of salvation" (Is. 12, 3). Then, carrying the water, the
priest in procession returned to the Temple through

the water gate and proceeded to the altar in the court of the priests, while the people waved lemon branches and sang psalms. Upon arrival at the altar of sacrifice, the priest poured the water onto the altar, whence it flowed to the ground. On the last or 7th day of the feast, the priests processed seven times around the altar.

It was precisely at this solemn moment on the 7th, the great day, as the procession passed him carrying the container of water that Jesus stood up in the waiting crowd and cried out with a loud voice, "If anyone thirst, let him come to me and drink. He who believes in me, as the scripture has said, 'out of his heart shall flow rivers of living water'" (Jn. 7, 37). St. John then interprets this extraordinary incident for us by saying that Jesus was referring to the Spirit that would be given when he was glorified.

This enables us to understand more fully now the conversation Jesus had with the Samaritan woman at Jacob's well. When he asked her for a drink and she gave him a hard time, he replied;

> If you knew the gift of God and who it is that is saying to you, "Give me a drink," you would have asked him, and he would have given you living water. . . . Everyone who drinks of this [well] water will thirst again but whoever drinks of the water that I shall give him will never thirst; the water that I shall give him will become in him a spring of water welling up to eternal life. (Jn. 4, 10–14)

Both times Jesus clearly refers to those who will be born again of water and the Holy Spirit in baptism.

It is in this context that we find the clues leading us to discover the amazing fact that it is we who are the successors of the Temple of the Lord—it is we who embody the promise of Yahweh that God's Temple will last forever.

We have seen Jesus equate the new Temple with his own body. But in baptism we become the Body of Christ, the Temple of the Holy Spirit, and the living stones of the Temple of the Lord not made by human hands.

The presence of God is within us. We are the Holy of Holies, the Tent of the Presence, and the Ark of the Covenant. The kingdom of God is within us, given to us at Baptism through living waters and confirmed and strengthened through the Eucharist where we, the Body of Christ, receive and are nourished by the Body of Christ, the Temple of the Lord. As Jesus says, "Behold I stand at the door and knock, if any one hears my voice and opens the door, I will come in to him and eat with him and he with me" (Rev. 3, 20). It is the Lord's supper, the Eucharist, that identifies and fortifies us with his presence.

And so the story of the Temple of the Lord goes on even as we go on, and the God of glory remains yet enthroned on the praises of his people.

There are two other story tellers who must be heard before we conclude this tale of the Temple; St. Paul and St. Peter. In one of the earliest books of the New Testament, written to the people of Corinth in the year 55, St. Paul speaks very clearly about the Temple. He is evidently referring to what had already become, by this time, a very clear teaching in the Church.

> Do you not know that you are God's temple and that God's Spirit dwells in you? If anyone destroys God's temple, God will destroy that person. For God's temple is holy and you are that temple. (Cor. 3, 16 f.)

In case there is any doubt, St. Paul in chapter six of this Epistle repeats this remarkable teaching.

> Do you not know that your body is a temple of the Holy Spirit within you which you have from God, and that you are not your own? For you were bought with a great price, therefore glorify God in your body. (1 Cor. 6, 19 f.)

In the beautiful Epistle to the Ephesians written either by St. Paul or one of his followers several decades after 1 Corinthians we see the same teaching even further developed.

> So then you are no longer strangers and aliens, but you are citizens with the saints and also members of the household of God, built upon the foundation of the apostles and prophets with Christ Jesus himself as the cornerstone. In him the whole structure is joined together and grows into a holy temple in the Lord; in whom you also are built together spiritually into a dwelling place for God. (Eph. 2, 19–22)

Strangers and aliens were forbidden to enter the inner precincts of the Temple area. But God's household, now embracing all Christians, have themselves become the Holy of Holies, the enthronement of God's presence in the world. So, not only is each individual Christian the Temple of God, Christians also comprise a foundation with Christ as cornerstone, and are joined together to form one magnificent Temple, a dwelling place for God.

How beautifully St. Peter joins in the Temple story by exhorting us all to reach out and embrace our sacred calling.

> Come to him, a living stone, though rejected by mortals yet chosen and precious in God's sight, and like living stones let yourselves be built into a spiritual house, to be a holy priesthood, to offer spiritual sacrifice acceptable to God through Jesus Christ. (1 Pet. 2, 4 f.)

CHAPTER 2

Wisdom Built a House

*I will tell you what wisdom is and how she
    came to be,
and I will hide no secrets from you,
but I will trace her course from the
    beginning of creation,
and make the knowledge of her clear,
and I will not pass by the truth;
neither will I travel in the company of
    sickly envy,
for envy does not associate with wisdom
A multitude of wise men is the salvation of
    the world,
and a sensible king is the stability of his
    people.
Therefore be instructed by my words, and
    you will profit.*

                 —Wis. 6, 22–25

ONCE UPON A TIME, Wisdom built a house . . . but
wait! I sense her wanting to begin her own story—
even wanting to sing her song about it.

"I am from the Lord," she sings, while execut-
ing sprightly pirouettes, "and with the Lord I will

forever remain.* I know such things as the number of grains of the sand on the beaches and can count the drops of rain even as they pour through the heavenly floodgates. I can add up the days of eternity. I am the favorite of the Lord, and because I was created before all other things, I played at his feet and heard the fiat of his mind when he determined the height of the heavens, the breadth of the Earth, the depth of the abyss, and the erratic course of the butterfly. Only the Lord is wise, and I am made to her image and his likeness. He saw me and took my measure, poured me out upon all his works and lavished me upon those who love him.

"The Lord is my father and my mother. I love him and fear her with the awe of reverence, the wonder of discovery, the glory of exultation, and the gladness of rejoicing. I am ancient beyond all mortal calculation, yet I am created anew with each of the faithful in the womb. Among men and women, I have made an everlasting foundation, and I will abide with them faithfully. My delight is to dwell with the sons of Adam and the daughters of Eve. Do you desire me? Love the Lord with all your heart, take care of one another and the Lord will lavish me upon you.

"I teach my children, and I help those who look for me. Whoever loves me loves life. Joy fills those who seek me. Those who serve me minister to God the most high, and the Lord blesses their comings and goings. I take pleasure especially in two things,

---

*There are very few direct quotes from any of the five Wisdom books of the Bible in this story. The few direct quotes are printed with references in the usual manner.

and they are beautiful in the sight of God and mortals: agreement among brothers and sisters and friendship among neighbors.

"Happy, indeed, are the mortals who reflect from the heart on my ways and ponder my secrets. They dwell amid my glory when they peer through the windows of my house and listen at my doors. They occupy a superb lodging place when they pitch their tents near my walls and place their children under my shelter. I will come to meet them like a mother. Like a young bride, I will welcome them and feed them with the bread of learning. Listen to me, my children, and live."

Well, that is the song of Wisdom. Now listen to her story. She speaks and sings from her own house built among the sons of Adam and the daughters of Eve. It is a house of four stories. Wisdom has a solid foundation of three stories and she dwells in the penthouse of the fourth.

In the thirteenth century (after the birth of Christ) Wisdom inspired one of her favorite sons, St. Thomas Aquinas, to describe her dwelling place. He did it by describing the functions of the mind, which is, after all, where Wisdom lives. The first function of the mind, or the first foundational story of Wisdom's edifice is called by St. Thomas *Information*. This is the data gathering place for Wisdom where she stores all of the almost infinite facts at her disposal. She has a capacity for data that would make all the computers in the world blush a flaming red—even the black and white ones!

Wisdom calls the second foundational story of her home *Knowledge*. This is where she takes the data from her place of Information and organizes it. This place she calls Knowledge, because the Latin word for knowledge is *scientia* whence comes our word for science, which is simply organized data. Again, the worldwide computer community blushes for shame, because although their capacity for data (Information) is incalculable, their ability to come to real Knowledge is nil!

Next, we go up to the third foundational story of Wisdom's house. This is where she lives out the concrete implications of Knowledge; the place where she experiences the meaning of her organized data, where it is proved, felt, and understood. This she calls the level of *Understanding*. Realizing how important this level is in order to come to her and how often we neglect it in favor of merely data gathering (Information) and Knowledge (science or organized data) Wisdom pleads with us:

> Knowledge is the principle thing
> Therefore get Knowledge
> But in all your getting
> Get Understanding. (Prov. 4,7 KJV)

To dwell with Wisdom in the penthouse, we must spend some time in each of her three foundational stores, gathering data, learning sciences, and experiencing in our lives the fruits of our studies by experientially living them out. Only then, are we ready, with the help of God's grace, to ascend into the very dwelling place of Wisdom. Here we will see, as it were, with the eyes of God and learn the thoughts of the heart of God. Wisdom will bring us into the very center of the cosmos. We will see and understand all of God's creation, insofar as nature and grace can make this possible, from God's own point of view, with God's own understanding, and with God's love.

Is it any wonder, then, that people have come flocking to Wisdom's house seeking entrance? From the very beginning of creation, thcy have been attracted, called, invited, and summoned by that very God-shaped vacuum in their hearts by which they are imaged in God's likeness.

It is not surprising to discover that Adam and Eve were the very first to seek wisdom—but under a deception. Instead of recognizing wisdom and the gift of seeing and thinking from the eyes and heart of God, they were deceived into believing it was something they could gain by and for themselves. In some way, eating of a tree would make them equals to God. This is the meaning of the text in Genesis where Adam and Eve were forbidden to eat of the tree of the knowledge of good and evil. The serpent, (remember, now, he was a deceiver) said that if they ate they would be like God, knowing good and evil (Gn. 3f.). Eve saw "that the tree was to be desired, to make one wise" and she took and ate and gave some to Adam. They received, not equality to God, and not wisdom, but the fruits of deception—a warped life in a bent world. But, like the element of hope in Pandora's box, their children would desire, hope for, and be called by God to true wisdom. They would have, despite their woundedness and proneness to evil, that God-shaped vacuum in their hearts summoning them to completeness and toward understanding themselves and their world from a Godly point of view.

The history of humanity from this time on would be the process of advancing toward God. The great eras of historical achievements are significant steps in that progress. The disgraceful eras are steps backwards. This is not only true of humanity in general, but it is also true in the life of every individual who can make the claim of being one of the "poor, banished children of Eve!"

The Bible is, in part, a record of this process. The word wisdom, in thirteen different forms, is used in 58 of the 72 books of the Old and New Testament hundreds of times. The truly great men and women of the Bible are shown either as dispensing wisdom or as searching it out. Certainly one of the most significant of these people is Solomon, whose name has become synonymous with wisdom.

It may be that Solomon's truly great father, King David, dwelt largely on the third foundation of Wisdom's house; that of Understanding. Occasionally he would reach up to the penthouse of Wisdom but actually to dwell there, really to be at home there, was left, at least for a while, to his son, Solomon.

As you approach Jerusalem from the west, where the winding road ascends a few miles from the city, you will see off in the distance toward the east, a large hill, called by some a mountain. This mountain was named by the Crusaders, the Mountain of Joy, because from it, away in the distance, those weary knights caught their first glimpse of the Holy City of Jerusalem. From the highway, a grove of trees can be seen as well as the outline of a building. Today this building is used as a home of worship by both Jews and Muslims—both for the same reason. In

The Temple of the Lord and Other Stories • 53

Solomon's day, the mountain was called Gibeon, and it was the place where he had his wonderful dream.

It was Solomon's custom, following the example of his father, David, to burn incense and offer sacrifice at the high places. This was permitted before he built the Temple in Jerusalem. Gibeon was the greatest of the high places, and Solomon had even offered as many as a thousand burnt offerings upon the altar there. One night when Solomon was sleeping at the Gibeon Temple, God appeared to him in a dream and promised to give him whatever he asked. Solomon, at this time, was only about twenty years old.

Showing that he already had a firm grasp of what he was requesting, Solomon thanked God for being so gracious to his father, David, and also for giving David a son to sit upon his throne. Then he added, "But I am only a little child and do not know how to carry out my duties . . . so give your servant a discerning heart to govern your people and to distinguish between right and wrong" (1 Kgs. 3, 7). This is what Adam and Eve thought to gain for themselves by eating from a tree. Solomon knew it could only come as a gift from God.

> The Lord was pleased that Solomon had asked for this. So God said to him, "Since you asked for this and not for long life or wealth . . . but for discernment in administering justice, I will do what you have asked. I will give you a wise and discerning heart, so that there will never have been anyone like you, nor will there ever be. Moreover, I will give you what you have not asked for—both riches and honor—so that in your lifetime you will have no equal among kings."

It would not be out of place here to rush ahead momentarily in our story of Wisdom to hear God make this promise again through his son, Jesus Christ: "Seek first his kingdom and his righteousness, and all these [material] things will be given to you as well. Therefore do not worry about tomorrow . . ." (Mt. 6, 33–34).

At any rate, Solomon awoke, and, behold, it was a dream! The reality, however, of this great gift of wisdom became quickly apparent when Solomon returned to Jerusalem. His famous judgment regarding the two prostitutes, each claiming the same child, was his first official action the next day. Truly, he showed the very wisdom of God by giving the disputed child to the woman whose heart yearned for her son even enough to give him up for his own sake.

Solomon's role as the symbolic master of wisdom and the cosmopolitan nature of his realm help us to discover one of the routes Wisdom traveled in her journeys around the Earth. She came to Solomon's court via his diplomatic relations (including his many marriages) with the court of the Pharaoh in Egypt. The schools attached to the courts of Israel and Egypt for the training of young noblemen as future diplomats became the delight of Wisdom who used them to reflect her many splendored facets.

She even dared to express her knowledge and understanding of God with the symbols, rituals, and traditions of religion. God's entire world is the source of Wisdom's insights. She did not need to experience the environmental crisis of the late twentieth century to understand the role of men and women living out their destinies in their highly existential, dynamic relationships with the whole realm of creation. Using Job as a mouthpiece, Wisdom tells us:

> But ask the animals and they will teach you, or the birds of the air and they will tell you; or speak to the earth and it will teach you, or let the fish of the sea inform you. Which of these does not know that the hand of the Lord has done this? (Job 12, 7–9)

Much of her sage advice even came from the simple homes of the people of the land or the shops of the common artisans. Often, it is a shared experience of the elderly to the youngster given, at first, orally and representing their legacy about life and living.

> My son, keep your father's commands and do not forsake your mother's teaching. Bind them upon your heart forever: fasten them around your neck. When you walk they will guide you: when you sleep they will watch over you: when you wake, they will speak to you. (Pr. 6, 20–22)

Wisdom, however, has no limitations and embraces the profound as well as the simple. She can be found in the huts of the poor and in the palaces of kings; in the workshops of craftsmen and in the lecture halls of philosophers. She deals with the most profound speculations on the creation of the world and the very nature of God and even with the inability of men and women to come up with adequate answers to these great mysteries. Sarcastically, God questions Job:

Where were you when I laid the earth's founda-
tions? Tell me, if you understand. Who marked
off its dimensions? Surely you know! Who
stretched a measuring line across it? On what
were its footings set or who laid its cornerstone
while the morning stars sang together and all the
angels shouted for joy? . . . Have you compre-
hended the expanse of the earth? Declare, if you
know all this. (Jb. ch. 38)

Wisdom, through God's grace, has chosen to
crystallize her teachings in a very special way in five
books of the bible. Because of his special relationship
to Wisdom, three of these books are attributed to
Solomon. No doubt parts of them can be traced to
this wise king, but reading them will show that they
are collections from many sources.

Wisdom herself tells us to be attentive to her
and to incline our ears to her understanding. We will
look briefly at each of these books so that you may
taste and see that the Lord is good. Then, when you
have partaken of these appetizers, you may desire
the entire banquet by reading these books yourself.

The book of Proverbs is an amazing but beautiful
and profoundly wise collection of instructions coming
from a tradition thousands of years old. Part of it is
modeled on an Egyptian book of Wisdom going back
some three thousand years. It appeals to lessons of
personal experience rather than admonitions and
instructions from the Torah or other religious books.
Nonetheless, its lessons on moral probity are based on
Wisdom's relation to God. Many have considered its
last chapter (ch. 31) as one of its most beautiful. It
speaks of "the good wife" and describes her status of

honor and praises her for being "far more precious than jewels," industrious in providing for the needs of her household, considerate of the poor, and honored by her children and husband. However, because Wisdom is not afraid to critique herself, perhaps today she would rewrite this chapter from the point of view of the woman rather than the husband.

Something of the exquisite beauty of the book of Proverbs can be discerned in just these few lines from chapters eight and nine.

> Now then, my children listen to me; blessed are those who keep my ways. Listen to my instruction and be wise, do not ignore it. Blessed is the man who listens to me, watching daily at my doors, waiting at my doorway. For whoever finds me finds life and receives favor from the Lord. But whoever fails to find me harms himself; all who hate me love death.

> Wisdom has built her house; she has hewn out its seven pillars. She has prepared her meat and mixed her wine; she has also set her table. She has sent out her maids, and she calls from the highest point of the city.

> "Let all who are simple come in here!" she says to those who lack judgment. "Come, eat my food and drink the wine I have mixed. Leave your simple ways and you will live; walk in the way of under-standing."

Would you like to partake of her sumptuous banquet. She invites you! Read the Book of Proverbs.

A very strange book indeed is the Book of Ecclesiastes, often called by the Hebrew name Qoheleth (The Preacher). The author claims to have been king over Israel in Jerusalem who applied his mind "to study and to explore by Wisdom all that is done under heaven. What a heavy burden God has laid on men" (Eccl. 1, 13)!

This book contains the reflections of a philosopher rather than the piety of the priest or the faith of the prophet. For him, God is in his heaven and his inscrutable will is done on Earth. We can do nothing but accept it. "I have seen all the things that are done under the sun," he tells us, "and all of them are meaningless, a chasing after the wind" (Eccl. 1, 14).

God has given men and women many things to be busy with, and whatever God does endures forever. There is good and evil, right and wrong, and they are all in the hands of God. It is idle and a chasing after wind for us even to speculate on them. His insistence on facing the realities of life (and death) are expressed in a masterly way.

> There is a time for everything, and a season for every activity under heaven: a time to be born and a time to die, a time to plant and a time to uproot, a time to kill and a time to heal, a time to tear down and a time to build, a time to weep and a time to laugh, a time to mourn and a time to dance, a time to scatter stones and a time to gather them, a time to embrace and a time to refrain, a time to search and a time to give up, a time to keep and a time to throw away, a time to tear and a time to mend, a time to be silent and a time to speak, a time to love

and a time to hate, a time for war and a time for peace. (Eccl. 3, 1–8)

The Preacher speaks of the skeptical side of Israelite wisdom. He does believe in God, in the fear of God, in a moral code, and in God's judgment on human behavior, but, like many of his contemporaries, he has no knowledge of an afterlife offering rewards or punishments.

He is open, honest, and forthright and very ready to quarrel with any theological teachings that ignore the reality of human experiences. Religion must be kept honest and in touch with reality. It is worth noting that this very attitude was one that the Church found necessary to repeat as one of the major shifts of theological attitudes in the Second Vatican Council. His teachings are summed up in the last chapter from an orthodox viewpoint.

> Now all has been heard: here is the conclusion of the matter. Fear God and keep his commandments, for this is the whole duty of men and women, for God will bring every deed into judgment, including every hidden thing, whether it is good or evil. (Eccl. 12, 13)

Although parts of it are considerably older than Qoheleth (The Preacher), the book of Job accepts his challenge to face the real issues of life. Wisdom, in this truly wonderful dialogue, frankly faces the greatest, most challenging questions ever to thrust themselves at the human race: the problems of suffering and evil, rewards and punishments, human freedom and God's omnipotence. Ambiguous about the answers, in the book of Job, Wisdom shows the value of asking the questions. Often, as in real life, the questions are more important than the answers. Complacency and denial are the alternatives!

Job should be read, at least once, in one or two sittings. This is necessary in order to follow its symphonic *leit motif*. A melody that possibly hints at an answer to the issues raised is played around and through the points and counterpoints of the arguments. At times, it seems clearly recognizable. At other times, it is the merest hint of a familiar echo promising more than it will give. The melodic lines of its polyphony, through the philosophical arguments of its speakers, create a melodic fascination by its contrary motion: one goes down, the other goes up; by its parallel motion: several orators take up similar themes and move together; and by its oblique motion where one moves forward in a straight line; whereas, others turn off in different directions. When you are finished reading Job, you will almost feel that you are on the verge of a solution to his problems only to discover that you must go back again and again to try to hear hints of a connected leit motif, which never quite seems to come through. Alas, the world must await the coming of Incarnate Wisdom in the person of Jesus to receive the answer to its problem of suffering—not a philosophical answer, but an experiential one! In a real sense, the problems of Job remain unsolved, and the questions must still be asked.

Almost certainly pagan and very ancient in its origins, the original story of Job is found in chapters one and two and in the final chapter (42). The intervening thirty-nine chapters represent the efforts of several philosophers, over a period of many years, to interject their own arguments, questions, and attempts at answers by introducing new speakers and even God into the dialogue.

Job, having lost his wealth, his status, his family, and his health bemoans his lot.

> After this Job opened his mouth and cursed the day of his birth. He said, "May the day of my birth perish and the night it was said, 'A boy is born!' Let that day be darkness! May God above not seek it, nor light shine upon it. May darkness and deep shadow claim it once more; may a cloud settle over it; may blackness overwhelm its light." (3, 1–5)

Small consolation is offered to Job by his so-called friend, Eliphaz who reminds Job that no one, not even he, can claim to be upright before God:

> A word was secretly brought to me, my ears caught a whisper of it. Amid disquieting dreams in the night, when deep sleep falls on men, fear and trembling seized me and made all my bones shake. A spirit glided past my face, and the hair on my body stood on end. It stopped but I could not tell what it was. A form stood before my eyes, and I heard a hushed voice: "Can a man be more pure than his maker? If God places no trust in his servants, if he charges his angels with error, how much more those who live in houses of clay, whose foundations are dust, who are crushed more readily than a moth!" (4, 12–20)

Another friend, Bildad the Shohite, does offer him some cold comfort. He tells Job that God does not pervert justice and he will restore Job's fortunes.

Surely God does not reject a blameless man or strengthen the hand of evildoers. He will yet fill your mouth with laughter and your lips with shouts of joy. (8, 20–22)

A small part of Job's answer to Bildad is worth repeating here.

How can I dispute with God? How can I find words to argue with him? Though I were innocent I could not answer him; I could only plead with my judge for mercy. Even if I summoned him and he responded, I do not believe he would give me a hearing. (9, 14–17)

It seems as if Job has given up! But has he? Read the book of Job, listen to his symphony and decide for yourself.

The two final crystallizations of Wisdom's teaching in the bible are found in the Wisdom of Solomon and in the book of Ben Sirach. Both of these books have been excluded from the canon of inspired scriptures by the Jewish community and the sixteenth-century Reformers. The Roman Catholic and Orthodox Churches, however, have accepted them from the earliest centuries.

The book of Ben Sirach (formerly called Ecclesiasticus; i.e., The Church Book) is one of the later books of the Old Testament, probably dating from around 200 B.C. It is similar in many ways to the book of Proverbs but prefers a smooth flowing poetry to Proverb's one-liners. It is the most religious of all the wisdom literature. In Chapters 44–50, Ben Sirach gives a beautiful account of God's dealings with his people in his hymn in honor of our ancestors, which begins:

> Let us now sing the praises of famous men, our ancestors in their generations. The lord apportioned to them great glory, his majesty from the beginning. There were those who ruled in their kingdoms, and made a name for themselves by their valor; those who gave counsel because they were intelligent: those who spoke in prophetic oracles; . . . all these were honored in their generations, and were the pride of their times. Some of them have left behind a name so that others declare their praise. But of others there is no memory; they have perished as though they never existed . . . but these also were righteous men whose deeds have not been forgotten. (44, 1–10)

Ben Sirach expresses a further development in the ongoing story of Wisdom. He identifies Wisdom with the Torah or the Law of God.

> Come to me, you who desire me, and eat your fill of my fruits. For the memory of me is sweeter than honey, and the possession of me sweeter than the honeycomb. Those who eat of me will hunger for more, and those who drink of me will thirst for more. Whoever obeys me will not be put to shame and those who work with me will not

sin. All this is the book of the covenant of the Most High God, the law that Moses commanded us. (24, 29–23)

There are many other embodiments of the Wisdom story scattered about the Old Testament especially in the Prophets and the book of Psalms. We shall look at one final phase of her tale in the Wisdom of Solomon.

This is the very last book of the Old Testament to be written, probably less than 100 years before Christ was born. This means, of course, that it could not have been written by King Solomon himself. However, it does embody much of his tradition and so rightly deserves the name Wisdom of Solomon.

The first five chapters of this wonderful book show a significant breakthrough in Wisdom's understanding of immortality. The Jews always believed in some form of life after death, but it was often in terms of a vague, shadowy existence in the underworld of Sheol. Now we see immortality as a gift of God to the righteous. The just ones are numbered among the children of God who stand before his throne and given the lot of the holy ones in his heavenly court. The ungodly ones say to eat, drink, and be merry because nothing awaits but annihilation.

Come, therefore, let us enjoy the good things that exist, and make use of the creation to the full as in youth. Let us take our fill of costly wine and perfumes, and let no flower of spring pass us by. Let us crown ourselves with rosebuds before they wither. (2, 6–8)

In chapters 3–5 we see the beautiful expression of immortality and eternal happiness for the righteous that shortly would find expressions in the teachings of Jesus.

> But the souls of the righteous are in the hand of God, and no torment will ever touch them. In the eyes of the foolish they seemed to have died, and their departure was thought to be a disaster, and their going forth from us to be their destruction; but they are at peace. . . . In the time of their visitation they will shine forth, and will run like sparks through the stubble . . . because grace and mercy are upon his holy ones, and he watches over his elect. (3, 1–9)

As far as fulfilling its purposes is concerned, the Wisdom of Solomon could have been written today. The authors' purpose was to encourage and strengthen the faith of the Jewish community living in the midst of a pagan society. Some things in this society were worthwhile, some were problematic. All had to be interpreted and seen through the Solomonic eyes of Wisdom.

The new society, which was the Hellenistic world, was exposing God's people to new facets of Wisdom and also to much that reflected her nemesis, Folly! An eclectic variety of religions and philosophical systems offered their own interpretations of the meaning of life, the way to salvation, and the pursuit of Wisdom. Suspicion of traditional values, skepticism, and a cosmopolitan influx from foreign cultures offered daily challenges. Many Jews had given in to the lure of pagan cults or secular philosophies. Those who did not were in constant danger of their subtle influences. Antisemitism was once again on the rise, calling forth the ancient question of God and justice, evil prospering and good suffering.

It was these issues that drove the author of the Wisdom of Solomon to the traditional scriptures of the Jewish community to search out answers. Through fruitful meditation, he brought hope and consolation to his people. He does not reject what Wisdom shows him is good in Greek culture. Indeed, he even uses it to show that true Wisdom embodies the best that the Hellenic world could offer. He offers to readers today undergoing similar conflicts that same hope and consolation.

Wisdom is a lady. She presents herself to us throughout her ancient story as a personification. She is not a person or a hypothesis within the Trinity, but a literary personification. She cries out in the streets, at the busiest corners, and at the city gates. If you seek her like hidden treasure, she will come into your heart and be pleasant to your soul. More precious than jewels is she, and nothing can be compared to her. Her paths are peaceful, and her ways are pleasing. Unlike the deceitful tree that Adam grasped, she is truly a tree of life to those who lay hold of her.

It was by Wisdom that God founded the Earth and established the heavens. It is he who gives wisdom and knowledge and understanding. Again and again does Wisdom invite all who desire her to begin the search. Again and again she repeats that the beginning of wisdom is the fear of the Lord. Fear of the Lord is the basis for following the Torah: "the

Lord commanded us to obey all these decrees and to fear the Lord our God so that we might always prosper" (Dt. 6, 24). "And now, O Israel, what does the Lord your God ask of you but to fear the Lord your God, to walk in all his ways, to love him, to serve the Lord your God with all your heart . . ." (Dt. 10, 12). Fear of God is the beginning of wisdom and is a condition of fidelity. "Be sure to fear the Lord and serve him faithfully with all your heart" (1 Sm. 12, 14). "And he said to man, 'The fear of the Lord—that is Wisdom' " (Jb. 28, 28). "The fear of the Lord is pure, enduring forever" (Ps. 19, 9). It is the foundation for praise. "You who fear the Lord, praise him" (Ps. 22, 23). It brings his protection. "The angel of the Lord encamps around those who fear him, and he delivers them" (Ps. 34, 7). It is, indeed, like possessing the Lord. "Fear the Lord, you his saints, for those who fear him lack nothing" (Ps. 34, 9). God loves those who fear him. "For as high as the heavens are above the earth, so great is his love for those who fear him" (Ps. 103, 11). Fear of the Lord begins with wisdom, because it leads us to follow his commands. "The fear of the Lord is the beginning of Wisdom, all who follow his precepts have good understanding" (Ps. 111, 20). Fear of the Lord adds length to life (Pr. 10, 27), it is a fountain of life (Pr. 24, 27), better than great wealth (Pr. 15, 26), and it teaches us wisdom (Pr. 25, 33).

It must be obvious by now that fear of the Lord is neither the craven fear of cowards, the trembling fear of the ignorant, nor the submission of the browbeaten. Rather, it is the awe of the wise who gaze upon the reflections of God. It is the response of contemplation.

Now, we come finally to the high point of Wisdom's story. She returns to her original home, which was at the feet of God but now with a difference. She makes her home with God-made-man, and finds her fullest expression in Jesus, and, because of our union with Jesus (in the Body of Christ), with our very selves!

It is not to be wondered at that wise men appear very early in the story of Jesus. Not having available the wisdom of God's revelation in the Bible, they utilized the wisdom of God's revelation in the world and in their own religion (probably Zoroastrianism) to seek, pursue, and find the embodiment of God's wisdom in the child, Jesus, at Bethlehem. So it was not only King Solomon who sought wisdom as God's chief gift to himself and his people, but it was also those Wise Men identified as gentile kings who pursued wisdom for the sake of the non-Jewish world.

There is, of course, in this marvelous story of the Magi another king. Herod is the embodiment of folly—the very opposite of wisdom. Herod was neither a Jew nor a Gentile, and any commitments he made toward the pursuit of Wisdom (the new-born King of the Jews) was really a commitment to self-aggrandizement, deceit, and fear. The folly of fools is deception (Pr. 24, 8). Herod would be a living example that "a man's own folly ruins his life" (Pr. 19, 3). Herod (Folly) rightly knew that Wisdom (Christ) would be his downfall, thus he sought unsuccessfully to destroy him.

The very earliest understandings of Jesus in the primitive church was as a Wise Man. This is called a Wisdom-Christology and is one of the earliest forms of Christological statement. Just as the sayings of Solomon and some of the prophets were collected as wisdom literature, so the sayings of the Wise Man Jesus were collected in much the same manner as, e.g., the Book of Proverbs, or the Wisdom of Solomon. Recent manuscript discoveries of the sayings of Jesus, such as the Gospel of Thomas, or even older collections, such as the "Q" source show this approach. In fact, the gospels, as we know them today, were probably based heavily on such wisdom collections.

In the gospels, Jesus is seen as the embodiment of wisdom. As a child, he grew and became strong and was filled with wisdom (Mt. 2, 40). His wisdom is even greater than Solomon's (Lk. 11, 31). His deeds, including his miracles, and his teachings demonstrated his wisdom (Mk. 6, 12).

Many of his teachings echo, repeat, or amplify passages in the traditional Wisdom literature of the Old Testament. Compare Jesus' teaching in Mt. 6, 12 on the Lord's prayer and forgiving our trespassers with Sir. 28, 2: "Forgive your neighbor the wrong he has done, and then your sins will be pardoned when you pray." Notice the similarity about his teaching of storing treasure in heaven (Lk. 13, 33) and Sir. 29, 10f.

> Help the poor for the commandment's sake, and in their need do not send them away empty-handed. Lose your silver for the sake of a brother or a friend and do not let it rust under a stone or be lost. Lay up your treasure according to the commandments of the Most High and it will profit you more than gold. Store up almsgiving in your treasury and it will rescue you from every disaster.

"Do not let it rust under a stone or be lost" certainly reminds us of the man who was given the one talent "who went off, dug a hole in the ground and hid his master's money" (Mt. 25, 18).

When Jesus spoke about the guests choosing places of honor and advised them rather to take the lowest places, we see an echo of Pr. 25, 6: "Do not exalt yourself in the king's presence, and do not claim a place among great men; it is better for him to say to you, 'Come up here,' than for him to humiliate you before a nobleman," And again in Pr. 25, 21 we see see an anticipation of Jesus' command to love your enemies (Mt. 5, 43f), "If your enemy is hungry, give him food to eat, if he is thirsty, give him water to drink. In doing this you will heap burning coals on his head and the Lord will reward you."

Let us, at this point of Wisdom's story, take it upon ourselves to answer the question asked in Pr. 30, 4.

> Who has gone up to heaven and come down? Who has gathered up the wind in the hollow of his hand? Who has wrapped up the waters in his cloak? Who has established all the ends of the earth? What is his name and the name of his son? Tell me if you know!

Scripture scholars agree that Wisdom left a song in the air in the early church that was caught by the author of Colossians who identified it with Jesus. It is worth hearing in its entirety as the early church sang it.

> He is the image of the invisible God, the first born over all creation. For by him all things were created:

things in heaven and on earth, visible and invisible, whether thrones or powers or rulers or authorities: all things were created by him and for him. He is before all things, and in him all things hold together. And he is the head of the body the church: he is the beginning and the first born from among the dead, so that in everything he might have the supremacy. For God was pleased to have all his fullness dwell in him, and through him to reconcile in himself all things, whether things on earth or things in heaven, by making peace through his blood, shed on the cross. (Col. 1, 15–19)

Here we see in a definitive and all-inclusive way that Jesus is the Wisdom of God. This fact is beautifully repeated in Heb. 1, 3–4.

The Son is the radiance of God's glory and the exact representation of his being, sustaining all things by his powerful word. After he had provided purification he sat down at the right hand of the majesty in heaven. So he became as much superior to the angels as the name he has inherited is superior to theirs.

This is why and how God loves us. It is his very own image and likeness he sees and loves restored to us by our redemption in Christ Jesus! The wisdom that Adam sought through the deceit of the serpent and by his own disobedience has finally been given to the human race by Jesus, who is himself the Truth and by his obedience even unto his death on the cross.

Where shall wisdom be found? Through your oneness with Christ in his body the Church, it is found in you.

CHAPTER 3

The Messiah of God

And what more should I say? For time would fail me to tell of Gideon, Barak, Samson, Jephthah, of David and Samuel and the prophets—who through faith conquered kingdoms, administered justice, obtained promises, shut the mouths of lions, quenched raging fire, escaped the edge of the sword, won strength out of weakness, became mighty in war, put foreign armies to flight. Women received their dead by resurrection. Others were tortured, refusing to accept release, in order to obtain a better resurrection. Others suffered mocking and flogging, and even chains and imprisonment. They were stoned to death, they were sawn in two, they were killed by the sword; they went about in skins of sheep and goats, destitute, persecuted, tormented—of whom the world was not worthy. They wandered in deserts and mountains, and in caves and holes in the ground.

Yet all these, though they were commended for their faith, did not receive what was promised, since God had provided

something better so that they would not,
apart from us, be made perfect.
                         —Heb. 11, 32–40

ONCE UPON A TIME, there was a Messiah of God. In fact, there were many messiahs of God. This is their story.

To be a messiah is to be anointed. This is the meaning of the word. Later, when the Hebrew word was translated into Greek, it became "Christos" and finally "Christ" in English. But with all its variations, it means to be the recipient of an outpouring of aromatic olive oil lavished on the head and poured down the face and beard. It is symbolic of richness, health, strength, blessings, and above all, of divinely bestowed leadership. It was both given to and creative of charismatic leadership. Indeed, even the word *charismatic* (as does the word *chrism*) means oil and ultimately anointing.

Along with such other obvious divinely bestowed blessings as water, bread, or wine, oil has been recognized and used as sacramental by many religions. It has been used as a symbol of life and holiness. Even inanimate things such as stones, sacred vessels, and buildings were anointed with oil to set them apart and reserve them for holy purposes. The benefits of oil to feed, heal, and even to beautify men and women ("... oil to make his face shine," Ps. 104) were transferred even to the objects used for worship.

In the Bible, we see that the first anointed ones; i.e., messiahs of God, were the kings. Among all the special things and people that called for anointing, none were as special as Yahweh's anointed, the reigning kings. Taking the custom, no doubt from their neighbors, the Canaanites, the Israelites anointed their king as their ritual of installment. For them, coronation was not the decisive factor that initiated one of their own into the royal dimension. Rather, it was the anointing, ultimately God-given, that elevated God's chosen one into the royal-divine family.

> I have exalted one chosen from the people.
> I have found my servant David; with my holy oil
>   I have anointed him. . . .
> He shall cry to me, "You are my Father. . . ."
> I will make him the first born, the highest of the
> kings of the earth. (Ps. 89)

Actually, it was Saul, as the first king of God's people, who was the first to be formally anointed as a messiah of God. "Then Samuel took a flask of oil and poured it on Saul's head and kissed him, saying, 'Has not the Lord anointed you leader over his inheritance?' " (1 Sm. 10, 1).

At this point in our story of the Messiah, we encounter an interesting event. We could call it the present influencing the past. Centuries after the reign of David, the concept of messiah was transferred back into Israel's history and given to her earliest leaders.

> When they were but few in number, few indeed
> and strangers in [the land], they wandered from
> nation to nation, from one kingdom to another.
> He allowed no man to oppress them; for their sake
> he rebuked kings! "Do not touch my anointed
> ones; do my prophets no harm." (1 Ch. 16, 29–22)

Thus, do we lengthen considerably beyond the kings the list of ancient giants, men and women, who were chosen by God as anointed (charismatic) leaders of his people. Names that we are familiar with from Joseph to Moses and Miriam are enrolled among the mighty messiahs of God. During the times of invasion and settlement of the Promised Land, the roster grows with the judges, men and women of amazing faith, prodigious deeds, and charismatic (anointed) leadership. Sharing in God's authority but taken from among his creatures, they showed in marvelous succession the strength of divine grace and the weaknesses of human flesh.

We could not do the story of the messiahs of God justice without at least briefly singing their praises and honoring them despite their failings. The Lord himself gave them great glory. They ruled, often in their own enclaves, within the people of God; made names for themselves by their own valor, by intelligent counsel, and through prophetic oracles. They were given honor in their own times and remembered in later generations. Some of them have been forgotten by name, but because they were godly men and women, the wealth of their lives remains with their descendents and their glory will live on (Cf. Sir. 44).

So we summon forth in our story the valiant name of Joshua, successor to Moses, who led God's people into the land flowing with milk and honey. We also call forth the judges whom the Lord raised up to deliver his people from the power of their enemies.

Among the first of these was Ehud from the tribe of Benjamin in the central region of the country. Oddly enough, about the only personal item we are told about him was that he was left-handed (Jgs. 3, 15). It was he who delivered his people after 18 years of subjection to the king of Moab.

There was peace in Israel then for 80 years. But the Israelites did evil in the sight of the Lord, and he delivered them into the hands of Sisira, commander of the Canaanite army. Sisera had 900 chariots of iron and oppressed the Israelites cruelly for 20 years. Then the Lord raised up the prophetess Deborah. She sat under a palm tree in the hill country near Bethel. When the people appealed for her help, she appointed Barak as her general and accompanied him into battle at Mt. Tabor. Sisira was defeated and fled only to be afflicted with an ignominious death by Jael, a Kenite and "of tent-dwelling women the most blessed" (Jgs. 5, 24), who drove a tent peg through his temple. So, along with Miriam, the sister of Moses and Aaron, we have two more women acknowledged as Messiahs of God.

The Lord chooses whom he will to be the anointed leaders of his people. Some of them were strange, indeed. Not the least among these was Gideon. He is presented as a hero of the tribe of Manasseh who ended the oppression of his people at the hands of the Midianites. A member of the weakest of the Manasseh families, Gideon had to be convinced of his calling by an angel. In addition there are elements of his story that lead us to suspect he was, in fact, half pagan. He delivered his people through extraordinary signs, divinely inspired battle plans, and dreams. His soldiers used the battle cry, "A sword for the Lord and for Gideon!" He was not the only anointed of God to compromise his messianic calling. In Gideon's case, he had fabricated a metallic idol, placed it in his home town of Ophah, and all of Israel prostituted themselves to it (Jgs. 8:27).

Another unusual candidate as a messiah of God was Jephthah. Called to deliver God's people from the Ammonites, he was the son of a Gilead and a prostitute. His half-brothers drove him away lest he inherit any of the family wealth. Collecting about himself a band of outlaws, he became so powerful that the elders appointed him as military commander to defend them against the King of Amon. At first, Jephthah tried diplomacy to bring about peace. Failing at that and determined to wage war, he made a vow to the Lord to sacrifice the first family member who greeted him upon his victorious return home after defeating the Ammonites. Although the spirit of the Lord was with him to win the victory, this promise shows a strong pagan influence. Tragically, when he returned to his home town of Mizpah after his God-given victory, the first person to greet him was his only child, an unmarried daughter. He acquiesced to her plea to have 2 months to prepare for her death and then sacrificed her according to the detestable ways of the gentiles.

Now we come to one of the most fascinating of the messiahs of God, the son of Menoah, Samson. The wonderful story of his birth was to be paralleled centuries later in the birth of Jesus. Samson was to be set apart in a special dedication to the Lord. When the angel announced his birth to his mother, he told her that her son would be a nazirite, one of a specially vowed group of spiritual men who separated themselves from others for service to the Lord.

According to the Book of Numbers (ch. 6), nazirites were not allowed to drink wine or even to eat grapes. As long as they wished to honor their special dedication, they were not allowed to cut their hair. Should they do this, their consecration as nazirites was over. Often a man would become a nazirite for a determined period of time for some temporary special reason. There was a ceremony fixed on by Jewish law to end the dedication. This involved a ritual shaving of the head after which the man was allowed to pursue a normal life.

However, in the case of Samson, his nazirite dedication was not to be temporary. According to the angel "the boy shall be a nazirite from birth to the day of his death" (Jgs. 13, 7).

Samson was called by the Lord to be a defender of his people against the Philistines. His strength was prodigious, and he was even credited with killing a thousand soldiers using as a weapon the jawbone of an ass. His weakness, however, was women, especially Philistine women. One of them, Delilah, was to be his downfall. To find the secret of his strength, she nagged him unceasingly day after day until he grew weary of it. His strength, he finally told her, came from his unshorn hair, a symbol of his nazirite dedication. While he slept, she cut off his hair and delivered him into the hands of the Philistines, who blinded and imprisoned him.

As a messiah of God, even in his weakness, Samson accomplished a decisive victory over his enemies. They brought him from prison to amuse them during a great feast day of their god, Dagon. Present in the temple of Dagon were all the lords of the

Philistines. Even the roof was crowded with three thousand onlookers. With one last burst of messianic strength, Samson toppled the House of Dagon "so that those he killed at his death were more than those he had killed during his life" (Jgs. 16, 30).

Not far from Samaria in the central hill country of Palestine was the holy city of Shiloh. Here, before the temple in Jerusalem was built, for many years the Israelites kept, in honored glory, the Ark of the Covenant.

It was here that Hannah, the barren wife of Elkanah, would present herself to the Lord each year to pray for a child. Finally Eli, the high priest of Shiloh, promised her that she would bear a son. Hannah pledged that the child would be raised as a nazirite and serve the Lord in the shrine at Shiloh as soon as he was weaned.

When she brought the child Samuel, which means "the name of God," to the temple, Hannah sang the beautiful song which was to become the model of Mary's Magnificat, even as Samuel was to become himself the model of Jesus's messianic calling.

> My heart rejoices in the Lord; in the Lord my strength is lifted high. My mouth boasts over my enemies, for I delight in your deliverance. . . . The Lord brings death and makes alive; he brings down to the grave and raises up. . . . He raises the poor from the dust and lifts the needy from the ash heap . . . (1 Sm. 2, 1f.).

So Samuel remained at Shiloh to minister to the Lord in the presence of the priest Eli and his sons. Now, both of Eli's sons were scoundrels and took unlawful shares of the temple offerings. Because of this, they were not to succeed Eli. Rather, it was Samuel who the Lord called by special invitation to be his priest and prophet. It is now in the life of Samuel that we see the role of leadership passing from the judges to priests and prophets and especially kings. It was to be Samuel's call to anoint the first Kings of Israel, Saul and David.

Samuel was also a judge over Israel and led them in victoriously routing the Philistines. He appointed his sons to be judges after him, but they were unworthy. The elders of Israel then confronted Samuel and demanded that he give them a king to govern them in the manner of their neighboring countries. It is at this point that Saul, a handsome young man of the tribe of Benjamin, who stood head and shoulders above everyone else, was called to be an anointed one, a messiah of God and the first King of Israel.

The custom of anointing a king, like the office of kingship itself, was taken by the Israelites from their neighbors the Canaanites, the Assyrians, and the Egyptians. It was primarily as a priest-king that he was anointed. This made him a holy person, not unlike a priest in character and function, who represented his people before their god. He was also assumed into the divine family, and the day of his anointing-coronation was his birthday as an adopted son of God. It was through him and his relationship to his God-father that the entire nation prospered or suffered.

Among the Israelites, at least in the beginning, the term messiah referred specifically to the reigning earthly king of Yahweh's people, a political figure with some cultic privileges and expectations. It was only later, closer to the Christian era, that the story of the Messiah of God reached out and projected messianic kingship toward the future and an awaited escatalogical kingdom.

So we are told that Samuel anointed Saul, who he found in the prosaic task of searching for his father's lost donkeys. Yahweh had told Samuel, "I will send to you a man from the land of Benjamin and you shall anoint him to be ruler over my people Israel. He shall save my people from the hand of the Philistines" (1 Sm. 9, 16).

As a messiah of God, Saul was to be numbered not only among his kings and priests but also as one of his prophets, siezed by the spirit of prophesy. Indeed, it became a proverb among the people, "Is Saul also among the prophets?"

Twice Samuel summoned the tribes of Israel together to acknowledge Saul as their king, once at Mizpah and again in Gilgal. He even recorded in a book the rights and duties of the kingship and stored it in the temple at Mizpah. Saul triumphed mightily over the Philistine army, but he did not observe his kingly duties as proscribed by Samuel. And so twice again at Gilgal, Samuel revoked Saul's kingship. The Lord regretted that he had made Saul king, because Saul turned back from following him and did not carry out his commands. It was neither the first time nor the last that a messiah of God would be a failure.

And now we must hear the story of David, a man of contradictions, a mystery, a saint, and a sinner, but, above all, a messiah of God.

The Lord said to Samuel, "How long will you mourn for Saul, since I have rejected him as king over Israel? Fill your horn with oil and be on your way: I am sending you to Jesse of Bethlehem. I have chosen one of his sons to be king." (1 Sm. 16, 1)

This is the first thing we must understand about the kingship of David. He was chosen by Yahweh. He had no blood ties to Saul, no leadership expectations in his own tribe, and was even the most insignificant among the eight sons of Jesse. He was the youngest and the keeper of Jesse's sheep, truly one chosen from among the people.

David was called to represent Yahweh before the people, but even more importantly, he was called to represent the people before Yahweh. As a king-messiah of God, David was the possessor of super human qualities. Indeed, as soon as Samuel "took the horn of oil and anointed him in the presence of his brothers, from that day on the Spirit of the Lord came upon David in power" (1 Sm. 16, 23).

This power David was given by Yahweh at his anointing was considered as constituting his royal righteousness. It belonged to all subsequent anointed kings and was to show itself in three ways.

First, the king was to be a warrior and a destroyer of Israel's enemies. David had already manifested this power. With only a slingshot and a stone, he struck down and killed Goliath, the champion of the Philistines.

Second, the king was to be a righteous judge over Yahweh's people. He was to raise the oppressed, give justice to the widow and orphan, defend the helpless, and protect their rights. Perversely enough, David was to act in this role even over himself as a persecutor of the innocent when the prophet Nathan accused him of killing Uriah the Hittite to get his wife, Bathsheba.

Third, the king was to be a conveyer of good fortune. He was to be as the light of the morning star, like rain falling on the new mown grass. Through him there was to be abundance of corn on every hill in the land. He was to bring fertility, a succession of good seasons, loyalty and contentment among his people, and the fear of God on every land.

The last words of David were to express these blessings.

> Now these are the last words of David: "The oracle of David son of Jesse, the oracle of the man exalted by the Most High, the man anointed by the God of Jacob, Israel's singer of songs. The Spirit of the Lord spoke through me; his word was on my tongue. The God of Israel spoke, the Rock of Israel said to me: 'When one rules over men in righteousness, when he rules in the fear of God, he is like the light of morning at sunrise on a cloudless morning, like the brightness after rain that brings the grass from the earth.'" (2 Sm. 23, 1–4)

The blessings and expectations that were associated with the king-messiahs of God were many. Although David shared in superhuman powers, he was a man taken from among the people. This element came to be stressed over his divine adoption. He was summoned by God and expected by the people to be the embodiment of the moral and religious ideals of God's nation. When he sinned, the whole people were infected and led to destruction. Time and again, we are to see in the subsequent history of the kings of Israel and Judah how king-messiahs did what was evil (or good) in the sight of the Lord and how, as a result, the people suffered (or prospered). Indeed, the king embodied the entire society.

The story of God's messiah next embraces David's son, Solomon. We have met him already in the story of Wisdom. Through his anointing and the outpouring of Yahweh's spirit he and all subsequent kings were attributed with a super-human wisdom. They were "lesser gods" (angels) and had the power to discern all things and to accomplish what Yahweh desired of them and of his nation.

As our story moves forward in history, we see that the line of king-messiahs stretched down the centuries from before 1000 B.C. to 530 B.C., Zedekiah was to be the last anointed king over Yahweh's nation. After a wretched reign of 11 years, the Lord gave him over to the Babylonians, who burned the temple of Solomon and destroyed the walls of Jerusalem.

Seventy years later a truly unusual messiah of God was to come on the scene. The heathen king of the Persians, Cyrus, was enrolled among God's anointed ones. It was he who issued a royal edict allowing the Israelites to return to Jerusalem and to rebuild the city and the temple. How beautiful is the oracle about Cyrus given in Isaiah. God called him by name, although Cyrus did not know him.

> This is what the Lord says to his anointed, to Cyrus, whose right hand I take hold of to subdue nations before him and to strip kings of their

armor. . . . I will go before you and will level the mountains. . . . so that you may know that I am the Lord, the God of Israel who summons you by name. . . . and bestow on you a title of honor, though you do not acknowledge me. (Is. 45, 1–5)

Indeed, they are messiahs of God whom God chooses and no man, nation, or religion can put limitations on God's selection!

It was the end of the kingly line in Israel and the messiahs belonging to it through the Babylonian conquest that introduced a brilliant new chapter to our story. The whole notion of Messiah of God hurtled toward the future. It was now the darling child of prophesy, the hope of the future, the expectation of God's mercy, and the fulfillment of his promises.

There are twenty-one passages in the Old Testament that speak of the hope of restoration of the Israelite kingdom through the advent of a messiah. These are all found in the prophetic books and date to some time after the Babylonian exile. It does seem that it was the demise of the actual, historical, messianic kingly office that gave rise to future expectations of an escatalogical messianic kingdom that would embody all of the divine promises of universal peace, sovereignty, and prosperity, beginning with God's people and eventually extending to the entire world.

Let us look at just three of these prophetic passages expressing this new concept of messiah as an idealistic future king.

Rejoice greatly, O Daughter of Sion! Shout, Daughter of Jerusalem. See, your king comes to you, righteous and having salvation, gentle and riding on a donkey, on a colt, the foal of a donkey. I will take away the chariots from Ephraim and the war-horses from Jerusalem, and the battle bow will be broken. He will proclaim peace to the nations. His rule will extend from sea to sea and from the River to the ends of the earth. (Zech. 9, 9–11)

This is what the sovereign Lord says. I myself will take a shoot from the very top of a cedar and plant it: I will break off a tender sprig from its topmost shoots and plant it on a high and lofty mountain. On the mountain heights of Israel I will plant it: it will produce branches and bear fruit and become a splended cedar. Birds of every kind will nest in it; they will find shelter in the shade of its branches. (Ezek. 17, 23)

For the Israelites will live many days without king or prince, without sacrifice or sacred stones, without ephod or idol. Afterward the Israelites will return and seek the Lord their God and David their king. They will come trembling to the Lord and to his blessings in the last days. (Hos. 3, 4–5)

When the exile was over and the temple and walls of Jerusalem were restored, there was a period of several centuries in which we know very little about the history of God's people. We do know, however, that their prophets and priests kept alive the promise of a messiah of God and his kingdom. After the conquest of the region by Alexander the Great, 300 years before the time of Christ, there was no place in Jerusalem for a messiah-king either according to the ancient Davidic model or to the future one.

The importance of the priesthood grew to a level hitherto unknown with the rebuilding of the Temple after the Exile. The distinction between king and priest became blurred with an emphasis on the priestly role. Now the high priest was seen as the Lord's messiah. The impressive vision of Zechariah shows this development.

> The word of the Lord came to me: "Take silver and gold from the exiles. . . . who have arrived from Babylon . . . and make a crown, and set it on the head of the high priest, Joshua son of Jehozadak. Tell him this is what the Lord Almighty says: Here is the man whose name is the Branch, and he will branch out from his place and build the temple of the Lord . . . and he will be clothed with majesty and will set and rule on his throne. And he will be a priest . . . and there will be harmony between the two." (Zech. 6, 10–123)

It may very well be at this time that anointing was introduced into the ceremony by which priests were invested in their sacred office. At first, it was only the high priests who were called "anointed ones," but later, ordinary priests were also anointed and thus received into messianic ranks.

When the Seleucids, as successors of Alexander the Great, forced Hellenic culture on the Palestinians (including of course the Greek pagan religion) in the second century B.C., it was a priestly clan, the Maccabees, who led the rebellion against them and introduced the last Jewish kings known as the Hasmonaean dynasty. Thus, there were messiahs of God who were both priests and kings. This was not unlike the ancient Jewish conception of the king whose cultic role was very important. The emphasis, however, now seems to be on the priesthood exercising an important royal role. It was just a small step from this that led to the expectation of a future messiah being both a priest and a king or even to two messiahs, one political and the other cultic.

Politically, socially, and religiously by the time the Romans conquered Palestine shortly before the birth of Christ, the atmosphere was ripe with expectation. Surely, now God would send the long anointed leader(s) of his people. This expectation grew out of the needs of a persecuted people. They did not heed the warnings of many of their rabbis who insisted that a messiah would come not when the people felt they needed one, but only when they were worthy of him. As a result, many false messiahs arose, enkindled a brief flair of revolt, were defeated, and left the people in a worse state than before. Such insurrections led to the final destruction by the Roman army of the city of Jerusalem and its Temple in 70 A.D. and then to the prohibition of Jews even living in Jerusalem after 135 A.D.

It was now the fullness of time, and God sent his only begotten Son as the perfect fulfillment of messianic hope. But according to his own model! God's Messiah was to be a king, yes, but his kingdom was not of this world. He was to be a high priest, yes, but one who has passed through the heavens, is without sin, and yet able to sympathize with our weaknesses.

Like the king-messiahs, he was called to be both human and divine, with an emphasis on the human. He was a man from among the people and at the same time Emmanuel, God-with-us. He was called to be the visible bearer and manifestation of the religious and moral values of Israel and a light to the gentiles. He embodied in himself the entire society, even as he incarnated the fullness of the Godhead.

His battles and his victories were to be against the forces of evil, which he showed at the very beginning of his ministry when he overcame the trials of Satan in the wilderness. He was the light of the world and the darkness was powerless over him. By his death and resurrection, he gave meaning to suffering. He came that men and women might have life and have it in abundance.

The true nature of his messianic role was not to be understood in his lifetime even by his closest followers, especially when it differed from the earthly triumphant ideas of messiah current in his day. He was to be the son of man, the suffering servant, who would:

> Have no beauty or majesty to attract us to him, nothing in his appearance that we should desire him. He was despised and rejected: a man of sorrows and familiar with suffering. Like one from whom men hide their faces he was despised, and we esteemed him not. Surely he took up our infirmities and carried our sorrows, yet we considered him smitten by God, smitten by him and afflicted. But he was pierced for our transgressions, he was crushed for our iniquities; the punishment that brought us peace was upon him, and by his wounds we are healed. (Is. 52, 2–5)

The stories of Jesus' baptism, temptation, and passion, as well as the infancy narratives are filled with messianic allusions. He is God's son in whom God is well pleased. He is a prophet who speaks for God. We are to listen to him on whom God's favor rests.

There are many texts in the gospels that teach of Jesus as the Messiah. It will be sufficient for our story if we look at just three of them. When he taught in the synagogue of his home town, Nazareth, Jesus read the messianic prophecy of Isaiah and referred it to himself. "The spirit of the Lord is upon me because he has anointed me to preach good news to the poor," and he said to them, "Today this scripture is fulfilled in your hearing" (Lk. 4, 20).

When the Baptist's disciples asked him outright if he was the Messiah, Jesus replied by stating that his actions clearly spoke of his messianic mission. He quoted from Isaiah again, and said to tell John how they could see messianic prophecy fulfilled in their presence "the blind received sight, the lame walk, those who have leprosy are cured, the deaf hear, the dead are raised, and the good news is preached to the poor" (Mt. 11, 5).

At Caesarea, Philippi, when he invited Peter's confession ("Who do you say that I am?"), and Peter replied by acknowledging him as Messiah ("You are the Christ"), Jesus affirmed his belief by telling him that his confession was inspired by God ("this was not revealed to you by men but by my father in heaven") (Mt. 16, 171).

Jesus' role as the Messiah of God was definitively established when he ascended into heaven to take his place at God's right hand. Here he exercises his messianic calling as supreme high priest. He is also king and is crowned with glory and honor. He was made perfect through his human sufferings in which he shared our lives and deaths. So he became like us, although he came from the fullness of God. Because he himself was tested by what he suffered, he is able to help us who are being tested. Thus, we who are holy partners in our own heavenly calling are united to him as the apostle and high priest of our confession.

> Therefore since we have a great high priest who has gone through the heavens, Jesus the Son of God, let us hold firmly to the faith we profess. For we do not have a high priest who is unable to sympathize with our weaknesses but we have one who has been tempted in every way, just as we are—yet was without sin. Let us then approach the throne of grace with confidence, so that we may receive mercy and find grace to help us in our time of need. (Heb. 4, 14–16)

The ascension of Jesus into heaven and the sending of the Spirit on Pentecost, while establishing in a definitive way his messianic call, does not complete it. This is a role reserved to us. If we are Christians, then we are followers of the Christ, the anointed one, the Messiah. This means that we too are messiahs of God! Truly, this is what gives our lives meaning. This is where we enter into the story of the Messiah of God.

Collectively, we are the Body of Christ. We are sons and daughters of God, like him and because of him God has sent the Spirit of his Son into our hearts crying aloud "Abba, Father." It is in the Messiah of God that we live and move and have our being.

Orthodox Jews still await the coming of a personal messiah of God, as do Muslims. Christians join them but await the Second Coming of the Messiah. Today, as you stand on the Mt. of Olives facing the ancient walled city of Jerusalem across the Kedron Valley, you can see a Roman arched gateway in the wall. This gate is known as the Golden Gate, but unlike the other seven gates to the Old City, this one is solidly bricked up. The tradition is that this is where the Messiah will appear to judge the world at the end of time. The bricks will fall out of the gateway, and he will appear there to summon the dead to resurrection.

Orthodox rabbis say that the messiah will come when the people are worthy of him. They claim that in every generation there are half a dozen potential messiahs; i.e., men who are anointed by God and who are graced to lead God's people to freedom and an everlasting kingdom. Any one of them is capable of doing this, but he has not stepped forth, because the Jews are not faithful to the Torah and to love of Yahweh.

Could not we Christians say the same thing? Only in each generation, there are more than a half dozen potential messiahs. We are all called, each one of us, to our own form of leadership by reason of our particular gifts given us by the Holy Spirit to build up the Body of Christ. And we are all given the greatest gift, the gift of love. It is going to be love that will summon Jesus to come again in glory—not the sins of the world, as we so often hear preached.

We are all messiahs, and the story of the Messiah of God embraces the life of each of us. We are anointed ones. Our ritual anointing takes place at baptism and confirmation by the holy chrism (oil) the bishop consecrates in Holy Week. This anointing we have received is a sign.

What better way to finish the story of the Messiah of God than to read the prayer of the bishop by which he blesses the holy oil that constitutes us as messiahs of God.

> God our maker,
> sources of all growth in holiness,
> accept the joyful thanks and praise
> we offer in the name of your Church.

> In the beginning, at your command,
> the earth produced fruit-bearing trees.
> From the fruit of the olive tree
> you have provided us with oil for holy chrism.
> The prophet David sang of the life and joy
> that the oil would bring us in the sacraments
> of your love.

> After the avenging flood,
> the dove returning to Noah with an olive branch
> announced your gift of peace.
> This was a sign of a greater gift to come.
> Now the waters of baptism wash away
> the sins of men, and by the anointing with olive
> oil you make us radiant with your joy.

At your command,
Aaron was washed with water,
and your servant Moses, his brother,
anointed him priest.

This too foreshadowed greater things to come.
After your Son, Jesus Christ our Lord,
asked John for baptism in the waters of Jordan,
you sent the Spirit upon him
In the form of a dove and by the witness of your
own voice you declared him to be your only,
well-beloved Son.
In this you clearly fulfilled the prophecy of David,
that Christ would be anointed with the oil of
gladness beyond his fellow men.

And so, Father, we ask you to bless + this oil you
have created.
Fill it with the power of your Holy Spirit
through Christ your Son.
It is from him that chrism takes its name
and with chrism you have anointed
for yourself priests and kings,
prophets and martyrs.

Make this chrism a sign of life and salvation
for those who are to be born again
in the waters of baptism.
Wash away the evil they have inherited from
sinful Adam,
and when they are anointed with this holy oil
make them temples of your glory,
radiant with the goodness of life
that has its source in you.

Through this sign of chrism grant them royal,
priestly, and prophetic honor,
and clothe them with incorruption
Let this be indeed the chrism of salvation
for those who will be born again of water and the
Holy Spirit.

May they come to share eternal life
in the glory of your kingdom.
We ask this through Christ our Lord.
Amen.*

Rites of the Catholic Church, vol. 1, pp. 711–12 (New York: Pueblo Publishers, 1990).